Becoming a Transformative Leader

MW00806635

This exciting book explores the concept of transformative leadership and how leaders can create learning environments that are academically excellent, equitable, inclusive, and socially just. Grounded in research and real examples, Dr. Carolyn Shields presents an approach to leadership that is engaged, authentic, courageous, and effective in addressing the needs of today's diverse student bodies. Featuring examples from schools and leaders, questions for reflection, downloadable eResources, and links to useful websites, *Becoming a Transformative Leader* is an invaluable and practical guide for school administrators, teacher leaders, and district leaders concerned about the uneven educational playing field for students in our schools.

Carolyn M. Shields is Professor of Educational Leadership in the College of Education at Wayne State University, Detroit, USA.

A companion title by Carolyn M. Shields:
Transformative Leadership in Education, 2nd Edition (Routledge, 2018).

Other Eye On Education Books Available from Routledge
(www.routledge.com/eyeoneducation)

Becoming a Transformative Leader

A Guide to Creating Equitable Schools

Carolyn M. Shields

Routledge
Taylor & Francis Group

NEW YORK AND LONDON

First published 2020
by Routledge
52 Vanderbilt Avenue, New York, NY 10017

and by Routledge
2 Park Square, Milton Park, Abingdon, Oxon, OX14 4RN

Routledge is an imprint of the Taylor & Francis Group, an informa business

© 2020 Taylor & Francis

The right of Carolyn M. Shields to be identified as author of this work
has been asserted by her in accordance with sections 77 and 78 of the
Copyright, Designs and Patents Act 1988.

All rights reserved. No part of this book may be reprinted or reproduced or
utilised in any form or by any electronic, mechanical, or other means, now
known or hereafter invented, including photocopying and recording, or in
any information storage or retrieval system, without permission in writing
from the publishers.

Trademark notice: Product or corporate names may be trademarks or
registered trademarks, and are used only for identification and explanation
without intent to infringe.

Library of Congress Cataloging-in-Publication Data
A catalog record for this title has been requested

ISBN: 978-0-367-20360-3 (hbk)
ISBN: 978-0-367-20361-0 (pbk)
ISBN: 978-0-429-26109-1 (ebk)

Typeset in Optima
by Deanta Global Publishing Services, Chennai, India

Visit the eResources: www.routledge.com/9780367203610

Contents

Detailed Contents

Figures

Preface

Becoming a Transformative Leader: A Guide to Creating Equitable Schools is a book for any educator who is concerned about the uneven educational playing field for students in our schools. You do not have to be in a formal leadership role, but simply in a position to make changes, to inform policy and practice, and to interact with others about how to transform our schools to ensure they are accessible and welcoming to *all* students.

Nelson Mandela once asserted that "education is the most powerful weapon we have to change the world." This book supports this belief, with the qualification that the weapon is only powerful if we ensure the inclusion and education of everyone—rich and poor; Black, White, or Brown; able or disabled; urban or rural, and so forth. This volume argues the need for education that is equitable, inclusive, respectful, excellent, and socially just. This book can and does stand alone, but it will be most useful when viewed as a companion to *Transformative Leadership in Education* (Shields, 2016). Despite the fact that the earlier volume gives some examples of transformative leadership and suggestions for implementation, many educators wanted more. They repeatedly asked for practical suggestions about how to get started and how to move forward as transformative leaders. This book is a response to these requests.

Overview of the Book

In this volume, you will first find an overview of transformative leadership theory (TLT), including a discussion of why a critically-oriented theory focused on equity, inclusion, excellence, and social justice is important. You will not find a lot of academic references or elaboration of theory, but once you have understood the basic concepts of transformative leadership theory, then here you will find many practical strategies for transforming your workplace or leadership preparation program. This book offers a practical guide; it does not provide a prescription. You will not find here a five- or seven-step program, but you will find some approaches that have worked for educators who have focused on creating educational institutions that are equitable, inclusive, excellent, and socially just. To do so, they have accepted the two underlying premises or hypotheses of transformative leadership and implemented the eight tenets identified in the following paragraph. The first premise is that when students are fully included and respected in schools they are better able to focus on their learning and academic outcomes improve. Second, excellent education requires a balance of both public and private good. The introductory chapter provides an overview of the theory and, because the full implementation of transformative leadership theory requires the implementation of eight interconnected and interdependent tenets, the tenets form the basis for each of the subsequent eight chapters. The tenets are:

1. Acceptance of a mandate for deep and equitable change
2. The deconstruction of knowledge frameworks that perpetuate inequity
3. The need to address the inequitable distribution of power
4. An emphasis on both private and public (individual and collective) good
5. A focus on democracy, emancipation, equity, and justice
6. An emphasis on interconnectedness, interdependence, and global awareness
7. The necessity of balancing critique with promise
8. The call to exhibit moral courage.

Following the discussion of the tenets, you will find a chapter written by Dr. Angelina M. Walker, a young bi-racial school principal who describes how she used transformative leadership theory to undergird her leadership of a turnaround school. The concluding chapter summarizes, once again, the tenets and the role of transformative leadership theory in the creation of equitable, inclusive, and excellent schools.

To support the implementation of these tenets, here you will find several kinds of resources including exercises you can use with staff and sometimes with students, examples from other practitioners, discussion and writing prompts, questions for reflection, and resources identified with either the eResource icon or with a link 🔗 to other useful websites. In the Introduction, you will also find information about how to access a survey that can give you baseline data about the extent to which you and your colleagues prioritize issues of equity and justice.

Of course, the ideas presented here are simply starting points and I would be pleased to hear from readers about any strategies you have found that work and about any particular challenges you have.

Who Can Be a Transformative Leader?

Any educator in a formal or informal leadership position, any teacher-educator who is called to a leadership role in any kind of educational institution, and any member of the general public who cares about the quality of education offered to all students can be a transformative leader. Moreover, you can live anywhere—a developed or developing country, an urban, suburban, or rural context. Transformative leadership is for you.

Many of the examples in this book and much of the data are from the United States because this is the context in which I live and work. Nevertheless, I have traveled widely and visited schools and talked with educators in many countries, and I am convinced that transformative leadership theory is applicable anywhere one can identify discrimination or disparity and that it holds the potential to offer the hope and promise of an excellent education for all students.

Reference

Shields, C. M. (2016), *Transformative leadership in education*, 2nd ed., New York: Routledge.

Acknowledgments

This volume owes its existence to the many graduate students and practitioners worldwide who have responded enthusiastically to the concept of transformative leadership and who have committed themselves to the difficult work of transforming schools to level the playing field for all students. I owe you all a tremendous thank you for your constant encouragement and enthusiasm.

The Authors

Dr. Carolyn M. Shields is a professor of educational leadership whose research and writing has, for several decades, focused on transformative leadership theory and the ways in which educators can address the needs of those students who are least successful and the most marginalized in our schools. One impetus for the work on transformative leadership was her early experiences with students living in a Grenfell Mission dormitory in Labrador who showed her the importance of meaningful relationships and how learning to understand the lived experiences of students could truly turn around their educational experiences.

Following the receipt of her doctorate at the University of Saskatchewan, Saskatoon, Canada, she ended her 20-year career in public schools and moved to higher education where her research has focused on how to create inclusive, welcoming, and respectful schools for all children with a special emphasis on those who traditionally have been minoritized and marginalized. The disturbing response of a teacher who explained that children would do better in school if they only had "better parents" still rings in her ears.

Dr. Angelina M. Walker is the author of Chapter 9 entitled *A Voice from the Field* in which she describes her work to create a school using the principles of transformative leadership. Dr. Walker's doctoral dissertation in which she also describes this process won the best dissertation award for the Leadership for Social Justice special interest group of the American Education Research Association. She is a Biracial African American and Italian mother of two children who leads a turnaround school in Denver, Colorado, and fights for academic achievement for all students through transformative, empowering, equitable, socially just, courageous lenses.

Her work focuses on empowering the community to build educational opportunities that result in academic achievement and to foster the qualities and characteristics of learners to create positive change.

For the past fifteen years, Dr. Walker's work has been predominantly with highly impacted communities of color in the Denver Metro area. She is deeply passionate about history and social justice as a means to drive critical thinking, equity, and change in order to redefine and expand horizons for future leaders. She holds a B.A. in Elementary Education, an M.A. in Linguistically Diverse Education (both from the University of Colorado, Denver) and a Doctor of Education in Educational Leadership and Policy Studies from the University of Denver.

The Work of Transformation

As this book clearly explains, the work of transformation is difficult. There are tremendous rewards but there are also many challenges. There are, of course, some who do not want the status quo to change; there are others who do not know how to move forward. We begin with ourselves, our whole beings—physical, emotional, intellectual, and spiritual. We need to be grounded, dedicated, and fully committed to all of our students, regardless of their backgrounds. And we must always remember that children do not choose their parents or their circumstances. For that matter, parents do not choose to struggle, to be poor, to be marginalized, unemployed, or destitute. For these reasons, we must offer hope and promise to all our students by transforming our schools so they fulfill the words of former first lady, Michelle Obama: "With an education you all have everything you need to rise above all of the noise and fulfill every last one of your dreams."

It is education that offers hope to all members of society for a better life lived in common with others. This book invites you to join with us in transforming both our systems of education and our society.

eResources

Keep an eye out for the eResources icon throughout this book, which indicates a resource is available online. Resources identified in this book can be downloaded, printed, copied, and/or manipulated to suit your individualized use. You can access these downloads by visiting the book product page on our website at www.routledge.com/9780367203610:

- Useful Web Links
- Experiences with Diversity
- Develop a School Profile
- Were the Chips Stacked Against You?
- Could You Live on the Minimum Wage?
- Alien Visitation Game
- Assessing Progress
- Goals of Education
- Discipline Role Play Activity
- Bloom's Taxonomy: A Pedagogical Aid
- Identity Activity
- Figure 5.2: Some important democratic pedagogical principles
- The Jigsaw Approach
- Conducting a SWOT analysis
- Images of School in Denver, Colorado
- Images of School in Monument Valley, Utah
- Developing Moral Courage: Getting Started
- Know Yourself

Introduction
Becoming a Transformative Leader

> "Effective" or "successful" leadership is critical to school reform. This is why we need to know what it looks like and understand a great deal more about how it works.
>
> *(Leithwood et al., 2004, p. 4)*

This is the question to be addressed here. What does effective leadership look like? There are many different theories and models, many books and articles identifying various leadership theories, many reform strategies, and yet, over the decades, there has been little sustained and significant change. Students from minoritized,[1] marginalized, and oppressed groups still fail to achieve academically at the same rates as their more mainstream peers. Black, Brown, Indigenous, and immigrant students are funneled into special education programs, low level classes, and remedial classes, in disproportionate rates. Likewise, students who are suspended or expelled are overwhelmingly from these same groups.

What kind of leadership makes a difference for all students regardless of their race or ethnic group, socio-economic conditions, sexual orientations and gender identities, religious affiliation, home language, abilities or disabilities? This book posits that transformative leadership theory (TLT) can provide some answers to this important question. It is a book for all school leaders who are faced with the challenge of transforming schools so that *all* students, regardless of background or home situation, may succeed. And most importantly, it is a practical book for educational leaders, in both formal and informal leadership positions, interested in transforming their schools in equitable and socially just ways.

Although this book can and does stand alone, it will be most useful when viewed as a companion to *Transformative Leadership in Education* (Shields, 2016), in which you will find a more thorough discussion of the strong research base for transformative leadership theory. In fact, if you want a book to use as a staff book study, then I would strongly suggest *Transformative Leadership in Education*.

In this volume, you will not find a lot of academic references or elaboration of theory. But, once you understand the basic concepts of transformative leadership, to be reviewed again in this chapter, then you will find here many practical strategies for transforming your workplace or leadership preparation program. This book offers a practical guide; it does not provide a prescription. You will not find a five- or seven-step program, but you will find some approaches that have worked for educators who have focused on creating educational institutions that are equitable, inclusive, excellent, and socially just. Instead, here you will find several kinds of resources:

- Exercises you can use with staff and sometimes with students, entitled "What Would You Do?"
- Examples from other practitioners to be used as a basis for dialogue
- Discussion prompts
- Writing prompts
- Questions called: For Reflection and Dialogue
- eResources, including additional activities to promote understanding and/or dialogue
- Links to useful websites with videos and activities

Baseline Survey Opportunity

In addition, if you would like to have your organization take a survey to identify how much their beliefs and actions align with transformative leadership, please send an email directly to cshields@wayne.edu. I will send you a link that can be used for your organization to access an online survey and, once it has been completed, I will provide an excel spreadsheet and scoring information. It may be useful to participate in the survey twice—once to gather baseline data and later, after you have spent time working with these ideas in your organization to determine whether there have been changes in mindset or practice.

What Is Transformative Leadership?

I begin with an overview of transformative leadership theory and an explanation of why it is important as a theoretical tool for transforming schools. Transformative leadership (TL) is a critical leadership theory that emphasizes inclusion, equity, excellence, and social justice. It is informed by James McGregor

> Transformative leadership begins with questions of justice and democracy; it critiques inequitable practices and offers the promise not only of greater individual achievement but of a better life lived in common with others.
>
> (Shields, 2011)

Burns' concept of transforming leadership as "a complete and pervasive transformation of an entire social system" (1978, p. 202) and by his subsequent statement that leadership's greatest task "must be to respond to the billions of the world's people in the direst want" (2003, p. 2).

Transformative leadership is informed by critical theorists who decry the inequities in the status quo and seek ways of redressing them. Thus, TLT responds to the persistent challenge of an "achievement gap" between students (usually White and middle class) who perform well in schools as they are now, and students (usually Black, Brown, poor, or non-English speaking) who tend to be less successful in existing schools. Rather than focus on an "achievement gap" that tends to place the responsibility on those who are not achieving well, we prefer to talk about an *opportunity gap*, or better still, an *empowerment gap* to emphasize the systemic and structural forces related to identity markers such as race and class that perpetuate inequity. Moreover, because these inequities occur in developed and developing countries, in rural, urban, and suburban areas, transformative leadership theory is applicable anywhere educators strive to create more equitable and more inclusive schools.

The Theory of Action

Transformative leadership theory is based on a theory of action that is informed by two general hypotheses. The first relates to individual achievement and the second to the collective welfare of a democratic society.

1. The first hypothesis is that when students feel marginalized, excluded, and unwelcome; or when they are worried about where they will eat or sleep, about the welfare of their family, or about whether they will be bullied or teased as they leave the classroom or school, they are unable to concentrate fully on learning. Hence, ensuring a safe, welcoming, respectful, and engaging learning environment permits students to engage more fully and results in higher academic achievement for all students. Moreover, no new program or pedagogical strategy will succeed over the long term until or unless this kind of safe learning environment is in place.

2. The second general hypothesis is collective and responds to the concept of education being both a private and a public good. It posits that when students are taught about, and prepared for, life in a democracy rather than simply prepared to pass a required standardized test, then the whole democratic society benefits. Too often, students are left to assume that democracy is simply a matter of each person exercising their responsibility to vote; however, a "one person, one vote" notion of democracy is much too narrow, given that the majority can (and often does) override the rights and needs of the minority. Hence, TLT adopts the concept of democracy described by Judith Green (1999) as "a society of mutual benefit" (p. vi).

To accomplish the desired transformation, Shields (2012) has developed a model of transformative leadership (see Figure 0.1) that includes eight interconnected tenets, all of which need to be intentionally addressed. In the following chapters, each will be described in turn, with a number of possible suggested strategies for moving forward. Moreover, given the need for educators to make data-informed decisions and to be able to demonstrate results, suggestions are offered for assessing the effectiveness of each strategy. For now, the tenets are simply listed here:

- The mandate to effect deep and equitable change
- The need to deconstruct knowledge frameworks that perpetuate inequity and injustice and to reconstruct them
- The need to address the inequitable distribution of power
- An emphasis on both private and public (individual and collective) good
- A focus on emancipation, democracy, equity, and justice
- An emphasis on interconnectedness, interdependence, and global awareness
- The necessity of balancing critique with promise
- The call to exhibit moral courage.

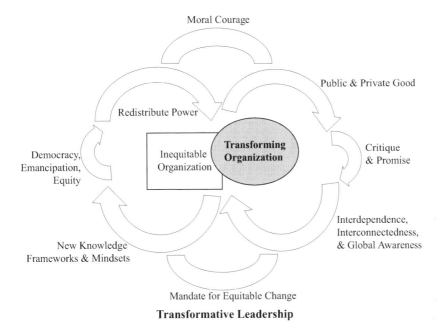

Figure 0.1   Model of transformative leadership.

Figure 0.1 indicates that the starting point for transformative leadership is an inequitable organization. A transformative leader then works through the various tenets, always in the direction of changing the environment, policies, structures, and curriculum to be more equitable and inclusive. Yet, as the model indicates, the work is continuous, and never finished, as the cycle repeats itself over and over.

Why Do We Need Transformative Leadership?

A few years ago, I found an image online that was labeled "Black Monopoly-funny" in which every square was captioned "Go to Jail" and in which the traditional space for Community Chest was entitled "Welfare." For this and other web addresses included in the list of live links, please look for the icon symbol. ⌥

There is nothing funny about that image that so clearly depicted the school-to-prison pipeline and in which the need for welfare is presented as a stereotype for all Black people. This led to my imagining a situation in which a group of friends who had been playing a game of Monopoly for about an hour, had purchased all the property and begun to build houses and hotels. If, at that time, another friend, an African American, came along and asked to join the game, what could be the response? If one player responded, "Sure. Pull up a seat. You can have the next turn," and passed the newcomer the die, what recourse would he have but to throw the die, pay fines, or go to jail. In other words, without some sort of redistribution of already purchased property, how could the newcomer participate on a level playing field?

In many ways, this incident is a metaphor for the lot of many African Americans whose ancestors were enslaved, and of many newcomers who, although well-educated in their home countries, willingly start from nothing to make a new life in a new country. Only 50.3% of the roughly 17,000 American students are White, with the other half coming from various ethnic and racial groups (CRDC, 2014). Yet data inform us that overall, Black and Latinx students have less access to courses that lead to college admission (calculus, chemistry, physics) and that they tend to attend schools that have fewer qualified teachers and resources than their White peers. A recent study of US educational outcomes found that,

> At grade 12, the White-Black achievement gap in reading was larger in 2013 (30 points) than in 1992 (24 points), while the White-Hispanic reading achievement gap in 2013 (22 points) was not measurably different from the gap in 1992.
>
> (Musu-Gilette et al., 2017)

As a society, we cannot morally or economically sustain these kinds of differences and claim to be a humane, caring, and progressive nation, especially when these and many other disparities related to achievement, attendance, discipline, college access, and more affect *half* of our young people. What a waste! How outrageous!

Although I am not suggesting that we should each give up some of our property and redistribute it, I am suggesting that we need to consider how our policies and practices, especially related to education, maintain an inequitable status quo instead of fulfilling Horace Mann's hope that education could be "the great equalizer." This must change and this book suggests that transformative leadership is one way to effect the needed transformation. (For my YouTube video in which this metaphor is reflected, you can go to www.youtube.com/watch?v=7YEsZNbfg-c 🔗.)

Why Not Simply Talk about Social Justice?

A quick glance at the eight tenets shows that what is outlined here is a series of principles grounded in the values of democracy, equity, inclusion, excellence, and social justice. They will look different in different contexts depending on which inequities are being addressed. In one context, poverty may be a dominant challenge; in another, trauma resulting from war, displacement, or refugee experiences; in a third, racism may be the dominant issue. There are no magic formulae, and no silver bullets, although the key is to identify and address the persistent, institutional barriers to student success that may exist in your school.

If transformative leadership is a critical theory that includes social justice, equity, and excellence, why should we not simply talk about leadership for social justice instead of focusing on transformative leadership theory? I have chosen this theory for clarity. Social justice is a phrase that can be used to explain conflicting and contradictory positions and hence, in some ways, means everything and nothing. For example, one could argue for building a wall along the southern border of the US to ensure the "justice" of keeping the country free from illegal immigrants, those who might take American jobs, and those who bring crime and drugs into the country. On the other hand, one can also argue vehemently, in the name of "justice," against a wall, asserting that refugees and asylum seekers have a right to present their cases, that immigrants have positively contributed to the welfare of this country, and that it is "un-American" to criminalize newcomers. In education, one might argue that it is socially just to mainstream a student with special needs to ensure he or she is able to become well integrated into the life of the school. At the same time, one can argue that the same student is best served in a self-contained classroom and that it is socially just to do so in order to maintain the well-being and safety of other students.

One reason for using the term transformative leadership is, therefore, that "social justice" has been co-opted by those on all sides of various arguments. Another is that TLT goes beyond many of the arguments of theories such as culturally responsive or social justice leadership in that it posits the need to understand how hegemony and privilege must be dismantled in order to create a socially just society. To express this more robust approach to leadership, I settled on the concept of transformative leadership theory.

Why is Transformative Leadership Important?

For decades, research has asserted the importance of strong leadership, or quality leadership—leadership that creates a culture of high expectations and school improvement. And yet, decades of reform efforts have failed to achieve their promise as thousands of students

> What separates successful leaders from unsuccessful ones is their mental models or meaning structures, not their knowledge, information, training, or experience per se.
>
> (Johnson, 2008, p. 85)

either drop out or are pushed out of our schools. One reason for the failure is presented by Johnson (2008) who posits that the beliefs and mental models of leaders have been largely ignored. Scholars have, instead, offered leadership theories that ask educators to hold conversations, to examine data, to identify goals, without providing explicit guidance about what kinds of conversations, goals, and data could make a difference.

Oakes and Rogers provide another explanation, asserting that "merely documenting inequality will not, in and of itself, lead to more adequate and equitable schooling" (2006, p. 13) and they assert that

> the vast change literature says little about strategies for disrupting social inequality through school reform. Theorists and change agents have not treated equity reforms as distinctly different from other school improvement initiatives.
>
> (p. 30)

They argue that

> a technical approach to equity reform falls short of achieving
> education on equal terms because privilege and exclusion are
> not discrete problems that result from ignorance, but rather
> ideologies that are endemic to the logic of much of the edu-
> cational system.
>
> (p. 15)

Thus, the failure of most school reforms does not lie in the failed or inadequate implementation of new programs, lack of decent school facilities,
qualified teachers, culturally and linguistically responsive curricula, and college preparatory programs (although these are all important), but in our
failure to acknowledge power, privilege, and cultural norms of exclusion.
These will be the focus of this book.

Change agents have generally assumed, as Oakes and Rogers (2006)
assert, that simply seeing the inequities will result in a desire to change them.
Yet they have neglected the issues of power and privilege, fear and resistance,
that prevent people from engaging in the type of change that is needed. If, as
Burns' argued, we need a "complete revolution of our social systems," then
there is understandable fear from those who benefit from the status quo, and
are thus reluctant to change it. This helps to explain why Oakes and Rogers
(2006) argue that "technical knowledge is insufficient to bring about equitable
education, even when attention is paid to changing the school's professional
culture" (p. 31). We cannot simply focus on the more superficial first-order
change without looking to the deeper second-order changes that can make a
lasting difference. Hence, we must accept the fact that

> Because of a political dynamic in which the existence, let
> alone the distribution, of power is never explicitly addressed,
> technical change strategies tend toward consensus rather
> than conflict. They aim at engendering a sense of ownership
> among all members, rather than a *fundamental realignment
> of advantage*. As a result, much reform energy typically dissi-
> pates in attempts to bypass or finesse explicit cultural struggle.
>
> (Oakes & Rogers, p. 32)

An Example

I was recently engaged in a conversation at a conference about first- and second-order change when a woman from Uganda gave this interesting example. She reported that in her high school, students had found the graduation mathematics requirement very difficult. Her math teacher decided to change the overall classroom environment by initiating a time of singing at the beginning of each class. Because students in her culture loved singing, math class began to be associated with enjoyment and stress was reduced. This enabled students to then approach the math concepts with a different mindset and in a more relaxed fashion. The result was that the whole class successfully met the graduation requirement in math.

First-order change may be small, but to be effective, it needs to have a long-term goal of sustainable and meaningful second-order transformation in order to be effective.

Can you give examples of first-order changes that may also produce more significant second-order change?

-
-
-

Transformative leadership addresses the failures in other theories head-on. It is not, and does not purport to be, neutral. TLT is not value-free, and it does not permit any educator or group to avoid the tough questions, the inherent cultural struggles, and the conflicts that must be addressed to achieve the kind of equitable, inclusive, democratic, and socially just schools that will lead to success for all students. Moreover, we have seen that when school leaders accept the need to address underlying assumptions, values, and beliefs, and when principles of justice and equity guide decisions and action related to human relations, fiscal resources, organizational structures, pedagogy, and instruction, change occurs. Generally, student achievement also improves without the need for costly after-school or noon-hour remediation, restriction of electives, narrowing the curriculum, or repetitive test-preparation classes.

For these reasons, and simply because it is the right thing to do, transformative leadership offers a promising, yet still challenging, way forward. TLT provides a lens through which to make decisions that can result in schools being more equitable and more inclusive of all students. It asks leaders to adopt the practice of asking the following questions when decisions are being made:

- Who is excluded and who is included?
- Who is advantaged and who is disadvantaged?
- Who is marginalized and who is privileged?
- Whose voices have been heard and whose have been silenced?

What Would You Do?

You, as principal, have a limited amount of money to disburse for new textbooks, art supplies, and sports equipment. You have a request from the art teacher for a kiln, from the head coach for new uniforms for the basketball team (that seems poised to win the district championship this year), and from the English Language Learner (ELL) teacher for supplemental reading materials in Spanish suitable for the age and grade level of your recently arrived immigrant students. You cannot do it all. How do you make the decision? What are your economic considerations? What are your cultural decisions? Are there any moral decisions? Try answering the questions listed previously.

What are the Expected Costs and Outcomes?

Scholars who write about leadership that is culturally responsive, socially just, or transformative have demonstrated again and again that when students are actively engaged in pedagogy that respects who they are and permits their involvement in co-construction of knowledge, they are considerably more successful than students who are subjected to what Freire called simply a "banking approach" to education—one in which teachers attempt to "deposit" information into their brains only to be withdrawn as needed for a response on a standardized test. Similarly, Parker Palmer (1998) rejected what he called the "inoculation" approach to education in favor of one in which students are actively engaged in questioning, and in sense-making activities.

We have previously indicated that there is considerable research that supports our claim that when systemic oppression and marginalization and the structures that support them are addressed, change occurs. When students are respected and included, and when pedagogy is relevant and engaging, student achievement improves and the "achievement gap" narrows. Additionally, when all students are able to learn about, and participate in, democratic educational practices, a greater understanding of citizenship, mutual rights, and responsibilities results.

Expect Conflict

However, as the previous query about allocating resources suggests, when there are decisions to be made that cannot satisfy everyone, conflict is likely to ensue. Each party in the discussion about the allocation of resources can make persuasive arguments about the need they have put forward. The art teacher might argue that having a kiln will give students who are typically disadvantaged and have few opportunities for creative outlets an opportunity to experience activities and find talent they otherwise would not have had. The sports director could argue that new uniforms will give all students, not simply team members, a sense of pride in their school and increase both student enrollment and enthusiasm for the school. And the resource teacher might argue that unless there are appropriate reading materials for the ELL students, they will never "catch up" and read with the fluency and sense-making required to succeed in more advanced studies. You will have parents and community members with strong feelings as well.

No matter what you decide, you cannot please everyone. If you buy reading materials, long-standing members of the community may well complain that the newcomers are taking resources away from those who have always been there and paid taxes. If you provide uniforms, there will be those who complain that you are prejudiced about newcomers, and perhaps accuse you of racism. And there will be some who argue that art is simply an expensive waste of time and does not result in better achievement on standardized tests.

The point is that exercising transformative leadership is never easy. There are personal costs and there will be pushback as you make decisions. There are no easy answers and it will bring valid and desirable positions into conflict.

Our response to the foregoing dilemma is that the money should likely be used to purchase reading books because it will permit fuller participation on the part of English language learners in the life of the school. Moreover, if the primary goal of the school is the education of all students to their fullest potential, then modified learning materials must be provided to those who need them and cannot otherwise participate fully. (But of course, one could build a similar argument for the other needs.)

Moving Forward: An Overview

In the following eight chapters, each of the eight tenets is introduced and clearly explained, and exercises and strategies are provided to help educational leaders to understand and implement each one. In Chapter 10, Dr. Angelina M. Walker, a school principal who has used transformative leadership theory to develop and open a turnaround school, presents a case study of some of the dilemmas she encountered and successes she enjoyed. This chapter will give readers additional practice thinking about how the tenets of TL both address and create challenges for those who are leading schools with diverse student populations. This case study is followed by a brief concluding chapter that provides a summary and some final reflections about transformative leadership.

In each of these chapters there are activities that may be used among educators to raise awareness and understanding. In some, there will be specific pedagogical activities that may also be used with students in classrooms. In every chapter, you will find information and questions that may be used to prompt reflection and dialogue on the part of educators. These will include stories to reflect on and discuss, free writing and dialogue prompts, resources that may be useful, worksheets, role playing strategies, puzzles, and other materials. These will vary depending on the tenet under consideration. There are, however, two strategies that undergird all others: reflection and dialogue.

Reflection. The need for practitioners to be reflective has been associated with Donald Schon's 1987 book, *The Reflective Practitioner* and has come to be associated with other concepts such as the development of a critical consciousness and with the fundamental quest to know oneself. Taking time to consider the implications of various situations, to explore the underlying beliefs and values, and to come to a determination of how one might respond to a given situation is an essential task of the transformative leader.

Dialogue. Similarly, dialogue is at the root of all human interaction. Note that *dialogue* should not be confused with *discussion*, which shares its roots with percussion and concussion. In discussion, one expends a lot of energy thinking about how one will respond and what one will say next, while in dialogue, the emphasis is on listening carefully and attempting to truly understand another's position. Defined not simply as talk but as a willingness to engage in deep listening and to remain open to others, dialogue is summed up by Russian literary critic Mikhail Bakhtin in this way:

> An idea does not live in one person's isolated individual consciousness—if it remains there it degenerates and dies. An idea begins to live, i.e., to take shape, to develop, to find and renew its verbal expression, and to give birth to new ideas only when it enters into genuine dialogical relationships with other, foreign, ideas. ... One voice alone concludes nothing and decides nothing. Two voices is the minimum for life, the minimum for existence.
>
> (1973, p. 71/213)

Engaging in personal reflection and taking time to share with others leads to creative, committed, and supportive relationships that are at the root of finding ways to transform schools in meaningful ways.

Please do not gloss over the needed time for these strategies.

Note

1 I use the term minoritized rather than the more common word minority or phrase majority-minority to emphasize that, even when a population is in the numerical majority, it can be considered "minoritized" because of the dominant power structures that continue to keep it in a subordinate position.

 References

Bakhtin, M. M. (1973), *Problems of Dostoevsky's poetics.* Ann Arbor, MI: Ardis.

Burns, J. M. (1978), *Leadership.* New York: Harper & Row.

Burns, J. M. (2003), *Transforming leadership,* New York: Grove.

CRDC (2015), *Civil Rights data collection: A first look,* accessed April 2019 at https://www2.ed.gov/about/offices/list/ocr/docs/2013-14-first-look.pdf.

Green, J. M. (1999), *Deep democracy: Diversity, community, and transformation.* Lanham, MD: Rowman & Littlefield.

Johnson, H. H. (2008), Mental models and transformative learning: The key to leadership development? *Human Resource Development Quarterly, 19*(1), 85–89.

Leithwood, K., Louis. K. S., Anderson, S., & Wahlstrom, K. (2004), *How leadership influences student learning,* Learning from Leadership Project, New York: The Wallace Foundation.

Musu-Gilette, L., deBrey, C., McFarland, J., Hussar, W., Sonnenberg, W., & Wilkinson-Flicker, S. (2017), *Status and Trends in the Education of Racial and Ethnic Groups 2017* (NCES 2017-051). U.S. Department of Education, National Center for Educational Statistics, Washington, DC. Retrieved June 2019 from http://nces.ed.gov/pubresearch.

Oakes, J., & Rogers, J. (2006), *Learning power: Organizing for education and justice,* New York: Teachers College Press

Palmer, P. J. (1998), *The courage to teach,* San Francisco, CA: Jossey-Bass.

Schön, D. A. (1987), *Jossey-Bass higher education series. Educating the reflective practitioner: Toward a new design for teaching and learning in the professions*. San Francisco, CA: Jossey-Bass.

Shields, C. M. (2011), Transformative leadership: An introduction, In C. M. Shields (Ed.), *Transformative leadership: A reader*, New York: Peter Lang. pp.1–17.

Shields, C. M. (2016), *Transformative leadership in education*, 2nd ed., New York: Routledge.

Tenet One

Accepting the Mandate for Deep and Equitable Change

Transformative leadership theory asks leaders to begin by carefully considering whether they are willing to expend the effort and to take the risks inherent in striving for deep and equitable change.

In order to do so, leaders will need to

- Reflect on their own beliefs, values, and assumptions
- Examine data from their school
- Understand the community context—social, political, and cultural within which they work

For further discussion of the importance of context, you may want to refer to chapter 3 of *Transformative Leadership in Education* (Shields, 2016). Once we have spent time carefully reflecting on our situation and the needs of our community, we can determine whether or not we are ready to accept the mandate for what transformative leadership calls "deep and equitable change." This is the kind of change represented by the cover image of these books—a caterpillar going through the stages of metamorphosis to become a butterfly. In other words, this change is permanent and not easily undone.

In this and other chapters you will find some specific activities intended to help you reflect together on the kinds of changes needed and to begin to implement them. Strategies, such as journaling, free writing, and the use of dialogue, will need to be repeated frequently.

The Need for Shared Vision

It is important to recognize that although this kind of deep and equitable change requires total commitment on the part of the educational leader, it also requires that the vision and commitment be shared throughout the organization. Hence, once the leader or leadership team has identified the need for equitable change and accepted the challenge, all activities to be discussed here and in subsequent chapters may be used during staff meetings and professional development sessions. The key is to ensure the vision is embedded throughout the organization and provides the focus for dialogue, policies, and activities. A one-time injection may work for a flu shot, but it does not work as a means of transforming schools. It is not enough to provide one session about equity, inclusion, excellence, and social justice in a designated professional development session. Dialogue about these topics must be threaded throughout every gathering of teaching teams, committees, or full staff meetings. It must be intentional and ongoing.

Let's get started.

 # Understanding Yourself

To begin, you need to know yourself. What guides you? What grounds you? Are there values or principles so important to you that you might be willing to risk your job for them? You may find it useful to keep a journal of your reflections and ideas you wish to explore further.

Perform a Cultural Inventory

One way to start might be to do a cultural inventory. If you were asked to share one item that reflects your cultural identity, what would it be? Would it be a piece of ethnic clothing? A souvenir from a recent trip? Something passed down from your great-grandmother?

Experiences with Diversity

You may also want to reflect on your own experiences with diversity by filling in the following questionnaire and sharing your responses with someone else.

1. I first met someone from a different ethnic group when I was _____ years old.
2. In my third-grade class, there were _____ people whose skin was a different color from mine.
3. There are _____ members of a visible minority who work in my organization (or school, or unit).
4. Have you ever been made to feel that you did not belong? What happened and how did you feel? _____
    _____
5. Have you ever caught yourself saying something that unintentionally expressed implicit bias? Write about what you did and how you realized it. _____
    _____

Thinking About Your Name

Another activity that is sometimes useful for raising issues of privilege, inclusion, and diversity when in a group situation is to give each person a sheet of poster paper and some colored markers and to ask them to draw images that suggest the significance of their name. Give each person no more than 10 minutes to explain their drawing and then post them around the room for further conversation.

It is interesting to consider where names come from, especially perhaps the names of those who were former slaves. First names were "given" to them upon arrival in America, despite the fact that all already had names.

Surnames were not considered important and so, after emancipation, a number of former slaves took the names of their former owners. Some, like Sojourner Truth, changed the names they already had (she changed from Isabella Baumfree); and others felt compelled to adopt names to represent their new freedom. One former slave, for example, when asked his name, indicated it was simply John. When asked, "John what?," the response was "simply John" to which reply he was asked the name of his former owner. When it was suggested he should be called by that name, his response was immediate, "Oh, no, master lieutenant, please don't put that down ... I've objections to that ... It will always make me think of the old ways, sir, and I'm a free man now, sir." The result was that he was henceforth called John Freeman.

> Where does your name come from? What does it signify? Why is that important to you?

Reflecting on Your Beliefs

To begin this reflection, you might want to access the *Transforming Leadership Questionnaire* mentioned in both the Preface and Chapter 1. This survey is intended to provide information about the extent to which current beliefs and practices reflect a focus on equity, inclusion, excellence, and social justice and will provide a basis for reflection as well as for identifying progress as you move forward.

Toward Increased Understanding

When I was asked to bring a cultural artifact to a recent meeting, I was stymied. What could possibly clearly demonstrate my cultural situation, that of a privileged, middle-class, aging White woman. I was very sure that others on the diversity committee of my university would bring ornaments or garments that truly reflected their ethnic backgrounds, but how could I accurately represent myself? I thought about the time when I had been at a conference in Cyprus and attendees had received invitations to a reception at the palace that stated "dress: formal or ethnic." Since I had not packed formal attire, it was an easy choice. I would have to do "ethnic," which for me, of course, meant that I would wear the western clothes I normally wore. However, when I explained my choice to my colleagues, I was met with blank and confused stares. They did not understand that my everyday clothes were in fact my "ethnic" apparel. These made me further reflect on an article by a former colleague called *White is a Color* (Roman, 1993). In fact, often when I ask participants in professional development settings to identify some aspect of their culture they want to pass on to their children, most White participants seem confused, and ask if I am talking about their religion.

Ultimately, for the meeting, I created my own "cultural artifact"—a collage of images of my great-grandmother sitting in a long dress at the oars of her rowboat at her summer cottage, of my own grandparents (my grandmother a university graduate and my grandfather a banker and school board president), and my own parents—each generation surrounded by a multiage bevy of relatives enjoying the summer at the cottage. For me, there was no better way to demonstrate the privilege from which I come, and hence the responsibility I bear in the perpetuation of the status quo that advantages some (like me) and disadvantages others. Moreover, when I share my story, I emphasize my privilege. I also recognize that privilege has not sheltered me from trials such as illness or divorce. Nevertheless, it has given me tremendous advantages that I am compelled to acknowledge. And, when I think about my name, it is these images from my collage I also attempt to draw because I cannot escape my heritage. And yet, I am forced to reflect on the experiences of some of my African American students who recount that they cannot trace their ancestry as I am able, because most of their records were lost or non-existent due to America's legacy of slavery.

My own lack of experiences with diversity as I grew up often raises questions on the part of others about how I became committed to equity. Growing up in a Canadian town of about 10,000 people, I first recall meeting someone from another ethnic group (Chinese) when I was in eighth grade and it was not until I was into university that I met a Black or Brown person. There was no visible ethnic diversity in my school, although I can still close my eyes and see a large teenage German boy, wearing a shirt and jacket, sitting at the back of my third-grade class. How lonely he must have been and how I wish I could just talk to him and make him smile. My organization now is highly diverse, although our College of Education in a university located in the heart of Detroit could still enhance its cohort of African American and Latinx faculty to more fully represent our community.

When I think about feeling as though I did not belong, I also recall an experience shortly after I, and my then husband, a clergyman, moved into a manse in a town in Newfoundland. As I walked home from the store, a local man said, "You don't belong here, do you?" He then proceeded to ask my name and attempted to deduce my place of birth by saying, "No, you can't be from that community because they are Catholic." As he continued, I knew with certainty that for him, because I had not been born in Newfoundland, I would never belong. But for me, that experience was temporary. It was somewhat amusing and did not hit at the core of who I am. It was not a reflection of my skin color, my sexual orientation, gender identity, or home language (although I did think his accent was peculiar).

My early insensitivity to issues of belonging and exclusion still causes me embarrassment. I had grown up hearing the phrase "Indian giver," but had never given any thought to its offensiveness and origins. At one point, I taught in a high school with many wonderful colleagues including a First Nations man who was the school's art teacher (and a particularly good friend). One day this colleague had lent me a pen and then, when I was finished with it, reminded me to return it (I am terrible about remembering such things.) As I pulled it out of my purse, I caught myself thinking "Indian giver." Why did it come to mind? What did it mean and what does it mean when said aloud?

Did you think of common phrases such as "einey, meeny, miny, mo ...." or "gypped" or "spaz" or even "gay." Also check out the origins of the following: whitewash, basket case, sold down the river, welfare queen, call a spade a spade, jew down, or off the reservation.

Take a few minutes to identify some offensive terms you heard (or used) growing up and share your current response to them:

1. _____
2. _____
3. _____
4. _____
5. _____

All of my experiences and reflections have taught me how important it is to help everyone to investigate their own backgrounds, their assumptions, and their positioning because some of us have plenty of experience being marginalized, while many of us also have experience being the ones who marginalize—without even realizing it.

Once we have spent time engaging in the critically important reflection about who we are, we can move on to examine our contexts. Let's start with the school.

Understanding Your School or Organizational Context

Educational leaders are very familiar with the need for data. In fact, you likely spend a great deal of time filling out reports, analyzing test scores, and preparing budget and enrollment reports. But data can be useful for identifying inequities within your school as well. And if you discover that there are no major challenges, no glaring inequities, then you can likely stop reading right now. There is no need to accept a mandate for deep and equitable change if you are already doing everything right (although I have never yet encountered a situation where that is the case).

Collect Baseline Data

Some people (see Brown & Shaked, 2018; Skrla et al. 2004) call the kind of data collection I am recommending an "equity audit;" I have often called it a "school profile." The key is to collect some baseline data so you have an accurate picture of where you started, and what you have identified as key areas of equity or inequity. It will be useful to use these data as a basis for dialogue and also to assess your progress as you move forward.

At the outset, as you collect data, it is important to be aware of the distinctions between the commonly used term *equality*—which implies that everyone is treated in the same way—and *equity*—which focuses on fairness and may require unequal distribution of resources. Which is your goal?

Develop a School Profile

Here are some of the questions you can ask and data you can collect about your school.

How many students do you have in your school? What percent are African American? Latinx? Asian? Indigenous? Middle Eastern? Other? What percent are LGBTQ+? How many students and which ones are assigned to special education programs or have individualized education plans (IEPs)? Do you have a gifted program and if so, who is in it?

How many students live in poverty? (How many students are eligible for free and reduced-price lunches?)

How many teachers do you have and what are their demographics?

What intra- or extracurricular activities do you have in your school? Which students participate in which activities? (In other words, it is important to know if all your football players are Black and all your band members are White and to ask why.)

What is your overall student achievement? Which groups of students are meeting expectations? Which groups are failing to attain the expected standards?

Examine your attendance, discipline, and suspension statistics. Which groups of students are under-represented? Who is over-represented?

Conduct a SWOT Analysis

Once you have collected the necessary data, they can be a useful basis for ongoing dialogue with the whole staff because they can speak for themselves. Sometimes during dialogue about student achievement, people can fall into the trap (to be discussed in the next chapter) of deficit thinking—i.e., blaming the students, family, or a particular group.

Starting with the data can help to avoid finger pointing and blame and identify the strengths, weaknesses, opportunities, and threats presented to your organization.

S   strengths
W   weaknesses
O   opportunities
T   threats

What do the data tell you about what you are doing well? Where are there imbalances and inequities? Where are certain groups of students disproportionately represented—for example, are Black and Brown students disciplined more than White students? Are White students over-represented in gifted and talented programs? And so forth. Where are the opportunities for improvement? And where are threats for declining enrollment or for discontent?

What Would You Do?

You discover that in your gifted and talented (GT) program, 95% of the students are White. However, at the beginning of the year you have one Indigenous student, two Latinx girls, and one African American boy in the program. Soon the Indigenous student quits, shortly followed by the African American boy. How can you explain this? What could or should you do?

Engage in Free Writing

Throughout this book, the concept of free writing will be suggested frequently. I am aware of one school in which the principal asked teachers to begin each staff meeting by writing for five minutes. At first they resisted, hating the activity. But soon, as they learned how powerful it was in terms of developing understanding and generating new ideas, teachers began to suggest topics and to ask if the others could write a response to a challenge they had identified.

Here, for example, you might ask the teachers to respond to the question:

> Why do you think we have so few under-represented minority students in our GT program?

Once people have written for a few minutes, there are many different ways to proceed.

1. You may open a general dialogue now that there has been some individual reflection.
2. You can collect all the responses, summarize them, and use the summaries as a basis for subsequent conversations.
3. You may ask them to discuss in small groups what they have written.
4. You may have them crumple up their pages and toss them around the room several times, ultimately opening one in front of them and using it as a basis for discussion. (This keeps all responses anonymous and adults are surprisingly energetic about throwing paper.)
5. You may distribute the responses for smaller groups to consider at grade-level meetings, or committee meetings.

Discussion

Many of the responses may suggest that the White students are better prepared, or that the White students are the ones who applied for the GT program, or that it is the White parents who want their children to excel so they can get into university. Here, some prompts are likely in order: Are White students genetically more intelligent than others? Have we tried to encourage other students to participate? How have we identified giftedness? What if we changed our identification criteria? Are we using grades as a basis for admission and is our curriculum truly designed for gifted students or simply for those who have performed well in the past?

An Example

One curriculum director noticed that in her district of 2300 students (over 60% of whom were African American), the population of the gifted program was 100% White. She began to ask, "Are you telling me that we only have bright Caucasian children and we have no bright African American children and no bright Hispanic children?" Ultimately, she reinstated an ad hoc committee, conducted a study, revamped the identification procedures, and "low and behold we had African American kids qualify, we had Hispanic kids qualify" and so the program became more diverse and more representative of the whole student population.

Research has shown consistently that when teachers and parents are taught some of the characteristics of giftedness (highly developed curiosity, endless questioning, interested in experimenting and doing things differently, long attention span, advanced sense of fairness, etc.), they do a more accurate job of nominating and identifying gifted children than many tests.

In fact, in the previous situation, of a program with over 95% White students, it would have been important for staff to ask themselves how they were identifying giftedness, and how a single child from a particular culture might have felt excluded and singled out. Indeed, this is an excellent example of how a sense of not belonging can impede academic progress.

Understanding Your Community Context

Finally, as part of your initial reflections, it is important to scan your community. Where are your supporters? What resources are available in the neighborhood? Which businesses, non-profits, churches, mosques, synagogues, or temples are in the vicinity of the school? We often think about low-income neighborhoods or areas with high concentrations of immigrants as being impoverished; however, it is important to identify all of the positive resources that are available. As we have often heard: **People are our greatest asset.**

A Community of Difference

Sometimes we think in relatively narrow terms about community. We are aware that those who share a common interest are often considered a community, such as a community of runners or card players. Sometimes we talk about a neighborhood as a community; sometimes the term is used to refer to those who attend a church or a mosque. Yet, when we think about schools and educational institutions, it is important to recognize that we are thinking about a *community of difference*—one that is made up of people who do not necessarily share a common language, heritage, beliefs, or goals. In fact, it is the diversity of people and ideas that comes together within a school that can be its strength if we permit all voices to be heard and everyone to be treated with respect. Hence, a school as a community-of-difference is truly a learning community in which all members learn *with* and *from* each other.

Community Mapping

One way of getting to know your community is to engage in an activity that McKnight and Kretzman (1996) call "community mapping." They explain that "first, all the historic evidence indicates that significant community development only takes place when local community people are committed to investing themselves and their resources in the effort" (p. 2) and second, that "there is very little prospect that large-scale industrial or service corporations will be locating" in local urban neighborhoods. Especially in many low-income urban neighborhoods, we tend to think in terms of "needs" rather than "assets," with the result that we focus on problems: drugs, violence, poverty, homelessness, illiteracy, or unemployment. Community mapping takes a different approach. It identifies all of the local resources, or resources that are local but controlled outside the neighborhood, including vacant land, service agencies, home businesses, schools, libraries, and so forth. Making an actual map of the neighborhood with the school in the center can actually demonstrate the talents and richness of resources that are available near the school. (Creating the map might be a good activity for a class of students.)

Mapping the assets of a community is important because communities are not built on deficits, but rather destroyed by the kind of thinking that suggests the only hope is to "get out" and leave. Hence, neighborhoods and neighborhood schools must rely on local assets and capacities if they are to regenerate themselves and be successful.

After actually mapping physical resources, in their article called *Mapping Community Capacity,* McKnight and Kretzman include both sample maps and an extensive capacity inventory of possible skills one might ask community members about—maintenance and construction skills, childcare or care-giving experience, office work, and so forth *∂*. Knowing the resources you might call on will help you to accomplish your goals of rebuilding your school in more equitable ways.

Accepting the Mandate

Once you have spent time individually and with your school staff considering your own beliefs, values, and positioning, as well as identifying the equity needs of the school and community, you are in an informed position to make a courageous decision to begin the task of transforming your school culture and the learning environment for all students. This is not a task to take on lightly, but the rewards are enormous. When students and families know they are accepted, welcomed, and valued, they are able to commit to fully participating in all of the learning activities and decisions of the school community. In addition to challenges, you may have emotionally rewarding experiences, as did one school principal who had gained a reputation for working with, and respecting, homeless parents. In fact, several new families came to enroll their students, saying, "We know you don't judge us here and we know that this school supports and helps all families and students. We are so grateful."

Bring a transformative leader is both exhausting and gratifying work!

References

Brown, K. M., & Shaked, H. (2018), *Preparing future leaders for social justice: Bridging theory and practice through a transformative andragogy*, 2nd ed., Lanham, MD: Rowman & Littlefield.

McKnight, J. L., & Kretzman, J. P. (1996), *Mapping community capacity*. Institute for Policy Research, Evanston, IL: Northwestern University. accessed November 2018 at http://racialequitytools.org/resourcefiles/mc knight.pdf.

Roman, L. G. (1993), White is a color: White defensiveness, postmodernism, and anti-racist pedagogy, *Race, Identity and Representation in Education*, 71–88.

Shields, C. M. (2016), *Transformative leadership in education*, 2nd ed., New York: Routledge.

Skrla, L., Scheurich, J. J., Garcia, J., & Nolly, G. (2004), Equity audits: A practical leadership tool for developing equitable and excellent schools, *Educational Administration Quarterly, 40*(1), 3–13.

2 | **Tenet Two**
Changing Mindsets

Tenet Two of transformative leadership theory emphasizes the need to deconstruct beliefs, assumptions, and mindsets that perpetuate inequity and to reconstruct them in more equitable ways.

This tenet may be the most important and this chapter the longest and most difficult in the book because it draws on research emphasizing the need to address underlying beliefs, values, and assumptions in order to implement sustainable transformation. Unless we challenge beliefs that perpetuate inequities, beliefs we have often learned from childhood, institutional transformation is likely to fail. Too often, however, the temptation is to skip this step and to focus on technical solutions, including new sets of textbooks, new teaching strategies, new discipline programs, and so on. But we must understand the importance of beliefs, values, and assumptions. Johnson not only identified this important aspect of leadership but also found that, "with some exceptions those in leadership development have failed to recognize this" (p. 85). The focus on underlying belief systems is one feature that distinguishes transformative leadership theory from other theories.

> The difference between effective and ineffective leaders is their mental models or meaning structures.
> (Johnson, 2008, p. 85)

In this chapter, we will focus on strategies that help leaders to begin the difficult task of changing beliefs and assumptions. Here we focus on the challenges of tackling concepts that some actually deny, such as racism, implicit bias, deficit thinking, classism, racism, sexism, homophobia, xenophobia, and so forth. It is important to note that these attitudes are often inextricably intertwined; for example, the history of racism in America cannot be separated from the deficit thinking often exhibited toward Black and Brown children. Moreover, as we discuss implicit bias, it is obvious that it is not separate from a history of White privilege and supremacy or from the entrenched societal structures that perpetuate oppression and marginalization.

Here, the strategies previously discussed—reflection, dialogue, free writing, and the examination of data—are particularly good starting points. In addition, storytelling, items from the news, video clips, and sharing personal experiences, can be useful to prompt reflection and dialogue. What is important is to help people begin to understand that some of what we have been taught (either implicitly or explicitly), as the image in Figure 2.1 reminds us, is wrong; it denies other people basic respect, or as Starratt (1991) calls it, "absolute regard." We may, for personal or religious reasons, at times disagree with certain behaviors, but we must always, in public institutions, recognize the right of every person to hold different values and beliefs and yet, to be included and respected. That is the strength and uniqueness of a democracy.

Figure 2.1   Don't believe everything you think.

What Would You Do?

I recall an incident that was reported to me years ago when I was teaching a graduate class. A classroom teacher indicated that she had a child in her class whose parent was gay. Another child had been teasing and bullying this child, making it difficult for him to concentrate in class. Upon investigation, the bully stated that he and his family were opposed to homosexuality and because they had a right to their beliefs, he could tease the other child in the name of free speech. To my amazement, the teacher said that her principal had upheld this position and told her there was nothing they could do!

How would you respond to this situation? What should the teacher and principal have said to the bully and his parents?

Educators can certainly not permit any child to be bullied or teased, regardless of a claim of free speech, because the right of the first child to be educated in a safe and respectful environment cannot be abridged by the second family's prejudices. In fact, here it is particularly important to distinguish between *belief* and *action*. Regardless of whether we agree with a particular position or lifestyle or not, we must demonstrate respect and regard for the other's right to hold their beliefs; but this right must not lead to danger or discrimination that injures or marginalizes another person.

Understanding Implicit Bias

In recent years, the topic of implicit bias has often been contested as being a politically correct concept invented by some on the political left. Really? Implicit bias refers to bias that is subtle, unconscious, or hard to pin down and there are endless examples that come to mind.

Numerous research studies, for example, have uncovered bias against Black people in employment in the United States. In a University of Chicago study, researchers mailed thousands of résumés to employers with job openings and tracked which ones were selected for callbacks for interviews. But before sending them, they randomly added stereotypically African American names (such as "Jamal") to some and stereotypically White names (like "Brendan") to others. The same résumé was roughly 50% more likely to result in a call-back with the White name—despite the employers saying they prized diversity. This is an example of implicit bias (Bertrand & Mullainathan, 2003).

Another Example

In 2016, the story of physician Tamika Cross went viral (Wible, 2016). Tamika was seated on a commercial airline two rows behind a man whose wife was screaming because he had suddenly become unconscious. When Tamika rose to help, the flight attendant twice told her to sit down and buckle her seat belt. They lost valuable time because the attendant did not believe that the young Black woman was a medical doctor. When her story became public, many other medical personnel from visible minority groups came forward to report similar airline incidents.

Follow the link under Wible to the full article for additional examples of similar occurrences 🔗 .

Can you think of any times when you made an assumption about someone based on the way they were dressed or the color of their skin?

Addressing Implicit Bias

How can we address implicit bias when those who hold such positions are unaware of them?

1. One way to begin is by introducing some of the simplest "cognitive dissonance exercises" known as optical illusions, in order to demonstrate how we can mis-see things that are right in front of us. Many optical illusions are available on the internet and include such images as the

familiar "duck-rabbit" or the multi-legged elephant. Others include the unusual triangle image in Figure 2.2 as well as the puzzle in Figure 2.3. Do you see an urn or faces? To see both, your perspective has to shift. Talk about your perceptions to ensure that everyone understands how easy it is to "mis-see" something. Further, although we may be able to see each image in two (or more) ways, we can only see one at a time.

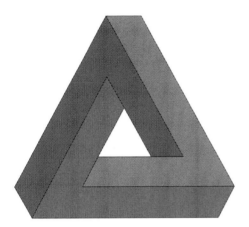

Figure 2.2   Optical illusion (triangle).

Figure 2.3   Optical illusion (urn).

2. Other ways to decrease the impact of implicit bias on decision making are to
   - Articulate your reasoning process
   - Use or create decision trees or other decision tools
   - Institute feedback mechanisms.

   If we are asked to *delineate our thought process,* we may become more aware of implicit bias and possibly recognize where we have made leaps of logic or reverted to emotional or political arguments.

   A decision tool, sometimes called a *decision tree,* is a graphical representation of the outcomes of various possible choices you might make. There are numerous videos on YouTube as well as models in word processing (often under smart art graphics) that help to explain how to create a tree in which one answer leads to a certain sequence of steps, while a different answer leads to different outcomes. Creating a decision tool with specific steps and criteria can also help to avoid thought traps that reflect implicit bias rather than explicit values.

3. Finally, asking others to give us feedback and to check our comments or decisions may be uncomfortable, but helps us to hear and see what others might see.

Eliminating Deficit Thinking

Deficit thinking is a hostile outgrowth of implicit bias. If we hold negative beliefs about a group of people, it is easy to quickly blame them for whatever situation in which they find themselves, absolving us of all responsibility. If there is one trap that can subvert all your efforts at school transformation, this is it. First, let's make sure we know what deficit thinking is. Blaming lack of achievement on the fact that a child comes

> Deficit thinking in education is a process of treating differences (achievement levels, abilities, ethnic origin, knowledge perspectives, etc.) as deficits that locate the responsibility in the lived experiences of children (home life, home culture, socio-economic status) rather than locating responsibility within classroom interactions and relationships, or indeed, within the education system itself.
>
> (Shields, Bishop, Mazawi, 2003, p. 16)

from a single-parent, or an impoverished home, or stating that it is because the parents don't value education, or that they don't care, are all examples of deficit thinking. Sometimes, the examples are blatant as when I asked a teacher what might help her students to achieve more academically, and she responded, "Better parents!" At other times, we may have to stop and really consider what has been implied in a given statement.

An Example

Think about the following situation! What is really being said?

I recently heard of a principal who, when discussing how to improve the reputation of his school, stated, "If we could only enroll more White students, our reputation would improve."

Here, the statement says that the lack of a good reputation for the school is because the students are Black and that if more White students—any White students—were simply to show up, the reputation would change. How is this an example of deficit thinking?

The research here is particularly compelling. As discussed further in chapter 3 of *Transformative Leadership in Education* (Shields, 2016), when Wagstaff and Fusarelli conducted research in 1995 along the Texas/Mexico border, they found that:

> The single most important factor in the academic achievement of minoritized children was the principal's explicit rejection of deficit thinking.

That sounds simple and it is particularly important because no new program or set of textbooks or teaching strategy will make a significant difference *as long as* we blame students and their families for their lack of success and fail to hold ourselves accountable. At the same time, of course, we cannot simply transfer the "blame" or responsibility from students to teachers, as though they are not trying hard enough either. I know of no teacher who gets up in the morning and says, "Hmm, I think I will do a lousy job today."

Address Deficit Thinking: Eliminate Blame

To address deficit thinking, a colleague of mine asks teachers to think about a student who is not achieving well. He then asks them, in small groups, to brainstorm as many reasons as they can for the lack of success. Once teachers have come up with many of the generally found reasons (parents don't care, lack of motivation, no place for homework, and so on), he asks teachers to locate the persons responsible by placing the statements into one of the following categories. (Add your own reasons to the following table.)

Responsibility of:

Family or Student	Institution (School)	Responsibility of Educator
Don't value education	Classes too large	Need cultural awareness
Lazy		
Too much partying		
Parents don't care		

Although it is true that there are some systemic factors such as lack of appropriate resources, or excessively large class sizes, it is also true that, regularly, approximately 85% of responses place the blame or responsibility on the student or family and less than 5% relate to educators acknowledging that they may not know enough about the student, they have not found out what his or her interests are, or they do not know enough about how to teach students from that social, linguistic, or cultural group.

The Chips Are Stacked Against Me!

Another activity that is useful to help educators explore their own deficit assumptions is what I call *The Chips Are Stacked Against Me!*

For this, I place a large pile of poker chips in front of each participant. Then I give them a list of what are generally thought of as adverse circumstances that prevent students from succeeding. (You may download one possible list from the web resources section.) This list includes such things as:

- I was suspended from school
- I had a parent or sibling who was incarcerated
- I come from an immigrant family
- I wore clothes from Walmart.

Participants are asked to quietly read the list and to place a chip in front of them for every statement that applies to them.

Follow-up discussion would include questions about why we associate these experiences with failure or with lack of ability. It is fascinating to discuss how and why those with the most chips became successful, and what factors contributed to their current success. Despite the fact that we often attribute many of these characteristics to parents or families that are not trying hard enough, I have found that most people attribute their success to their parents' determination that they should finish school because it is so important to their futures.

Addressing Race and Racism

Another belief that must be addressed explicitly is that of race and racism. Again, see chapter 3 of *Transformative Leadership in Education* (Shields, 2016) for further discussion and illustrations. Two recent incidents come to mind. One of my (African American) doctoral students recently recounted the following incident:

> While I was waiting at a hotel bar for colleagues to come down for dinner, I engaged in a conversation with a White couple. I'm not sure how we got on the topic, but I just remembered feeling shocked when the husband stated that racism no longer existed.

Another Example

This reminded me of an experience I had had recently as well:

At a major conference in a large American city, the female African American presenter came in and began by recounting her experience earlier that day. She said, "When I first got up, I was dressed in more casual clothes and was walking down the hall to go to the gym, when a (White) man came out of his room, saw me, and asked if I could get him some towels."

The contrast between the two incidents is striking. Despite a relatively common perception, racism does still exist. If I (a privileged White woman) knock on the door of an apartment building, I will not be told, because of my skin color, that the apartment has been rented. I am rarely, if ever, followed in a large department store by the security guard, fearing I may steal something. Moreover, I am unlikely to be subjected to the microaggressions recounted previously, or the employment discrimination identified at the beginning of this chapter.

Racism is real and is inherent in our assumptions and beliefs, in our values, and in the institutions and social systems of this and many other countries. Fortunately, there are many resources available to help us understand and address racism—another implicit attitude that also results in deficit thinking.

1. Some of these are on the *Teaching Tolerance* section of the website of the Southern Poverty Law Society 🔗.
2. Another useful resource is the website for James Loewen's (2005) book, *Sundown Towns*—a book that documents in vivid detail the persistent presence of towns which, after the brief Reconstruction period, forbade Blacks and in some cases Jews from living in them. The interactive map and other resources provide much food for thought 🔗.
3. Still, another useful resource is the series of YouTube videos that report on the series of experiments related to race and racism conducted in

2010 by CNN's Anderson Cooper and Soledad O'Brien &. For example, the video found at www.youtube.com/watch?v=EQACkg5i4AY is heartbreaking in that it shows that even young African American children demonstrate a belief that Whiteness is better than their own skin color. This is also apparent in several other videos in the series, for example, www.youtube.com/watch?v=Sm_CfET1Ffg in which a young boy identifies the darkest child as "dumb because he is dark."

4. Another helpful resource that may be downloaded from the web resources is Peggy MacIntosh's exercise called "White Privilege: Unpacking the Invisible Knapsack." This "backpack" contains a list of 50 items of privilege that most non-White friends and colleagues cannot share &.

5. Videos, stories from the newspaper, and personal experiences may be useful as a basis for thinking about racism and its impact on our schools.

6. Any of these resources may serve as prompts for dialogue, free writing, or role play. Think about how many people from another race or ethnic group you count in your circle of friends. If your curriculum does not reflect diversity, reflect on why. There is no doubt that concepts such as social inclusion theory remind us that we tend to attract and be attracted by those who are like us, but we must guard against negative assumptions and stereotypes about those who are different. See the story in chapter 3 of *Transformative Leadership in Education* about the principal, Catherine Lake, who threatened to put a banner on the front of her school proclaiming the differences in achievement by ethnic group.

Addressing Social Class and Poverty

Social class is a term that describes much more than poverty in that it represents a social construction of class based on advantage, education, material wealth, job/career, and so forth. At the same time, it is often simply equated with poverty, and once again, is the source of much deficit thinking and many erroneous assumptions.

1. Here again, the use of the *Chips Are Stacked Against Us* strategy is one possible starting point.

2. Another is to take the annual poverty rate data 🔗 and ask participants to plan their expenditures. For example, the 2017 poverty
   rate for the United States was set at $12,488 for a single person and
   $25,094 for a family of four. One could give participants a worksheet
   such as *"Could You Live on the Minimum Wage?"* and ask them to
   complete it 🔻.

Could You Live on the Minimum Wage?

You are the head of a four-person household and your monthly
income is $2091. Allocate your income in the best way possible to
support your family's needs.

1. Housing (rent) (Most people in lower income
   brackets spend approximately 40% of their
   budget here.)   _____
2. Transportation (car insurance, gas, repairs or
   public transportation costs)   _____
3. Groceries   _____
4. Personal and family care   _____
5. Health care, emergency room visits, dental care   _____
6. Restaurant meals and fast food snacks   _____
7. Clothes   _____
8. Entertainment, magazines, movies, plays, etc.   _____
9. School supplies, and extra activity fees   _____
10. Household items, furniture   _____
11. Utilities, phone costs, TV, etc.   _____
12. Travel, vacations   _____
13. Charitable giving   _____
14. Other (Do you have to pay taxes?)   _____

                                        TOTAL   _____

What would you cut if you found you could not make ends meet?
Where could you go to find help?

---

3. Other useful resources may be found at the website of the National Center for Children living in Poverty (NCCP) or at Scientific Learning's Fast Forward website 🔗.
4. Acknowledge that poverty can explain many of the gaps between a child's prior opportunity to learn something and his or her ability to learn. (Those familiar with *Transformative Leadership in Education* will recall the painting metaphor outlined on p. 129 that helps us to understand the difference between a child's ability to do something and their prior opportunity to learn something.) Moreover, IQ is not fixed but may be developed and changed by building children's cognitive capacity, helping them develop vocabulary, learn to ask critical questions, experience new things, and to fill in some of the gaps that their parents may have been too busy or too stressed to teach them.

Of course, there are different kinds of poverty with distinct characteristics and challenges. Someone who is a victim of "situational poverty," who may have recently become impoverished because of a serious illness or accident, or due to bereavement, or whose house has burned because of a rogue fire, will have very different needs from those who experience "generational poverty"—a persistent form of poverty that affects families for several generations. While those experiencing the former may have predominantly physical and emotional needs, those experiencing the latter may have those needs compounded by intellectual and educational deficits largely due to persistent, poor nutrition. The key is to know our students and their families.

I recently spoke with a well-established African American curriculum consultant who shared her own story of growing up in an impoverished family. She indicated that although they were never hungry, it was not until she was an educated adult that she had ever seen the inside of a theater. Her comment was that we must take time to try to imagine what circumstances children have not had the opportunity to experience. Her story reminded me of the second-grader I met in Florida who, when asked where he would most like to go, responded, "To Walmart, so I could have some new clothes."

We must constantly remind ourselves that *children do not choose their families or their circumstances.* They do not have control over their parents' health, their habits, or whether or not there is disposable income for new clothes or books or vacations (let alone a trip to Walmart.) But we, as educators, are responsible for educating every child, building on their curiosity, and helping them increase their IQ. This is important because research has shown that children from poverty must make *at least* 1.5 years of progress in an academic year in order to succeed and remain in school.

One thing educators must not do, as some writers such as Ruby Payne (1995) have suggested, is communicate to students that they must reject their family or their culture in order to be successful. In fact, this mindset reflects deficit thinking about those who live in poverty, often through no fault of their own, and implies that theirs is a kind of negative or lesser sub-culture.[1]

> ## Getting to Know Our Students
>
> Who are our impoverished or our homeless children and how can we address their needs?
>
> Who is experiencing situational poverty and how can we address their needs?
>
> Who is a victim of generational poverty and how can we address their needs?
>
> And in every case, what should we not do?

Addressing Sexual Orientation, Gender Identity, and Belonging (and Eliminating Homophobia)

Statistics tell a disturbing tale about the success of children and youth who are not, or do not present, as heteronormative. We know that over 18% of students are either homosexual or questioning or have a family member who identifies as gay, lesbian, or transgender. GLSEN's 2017 National School Climate Survey reports that, although the educational climate for LGBTQ+ students is improving overall, progress has slowed (Kosciw et al., 2018). "59.5% of LGBTQ students felt unsafe at school because of their sexual orientation, 44.6% because of their gender expression, and 35.0% because of their gender" (p. xviii). In addition, most (75.4%) reported either being unwelcome or avoiding school functions because they felt unsafe or uncomfortable and 18% reported having changed schools due to feeling unsafe or uncomfortable at school. And of course, as educators, we are aware of the negative impact of changing schools on student attendance, achievement, and graduation rates. Perhaps even more disturbing is the role of educators in that "56.6% of students reported hearing homophobic remarks from their teachers or other school staff, and 71.0% of students reported hearing negative remarks about gender expression from teachers or other school staff."

For transgender students, the situation is often worse. Statistics tell us repeatedly that of those who are not supported or permitted to "transition," 41% attempt suicide. Many parents of transgender children report that once they took the *persistent, insistent,* and *consistent* urging of their child seriously, that child changed overnight from being depressed and worried to being happy and well-adjusted. *&* Links to some YouTube videos that tell their stories are excellent starting points for conversation with educator and parent groups, and are included in the eResource list of web links.

What Would You Do?

One of my graduate students told me that a child in her primary school class had identified as transgender and that her school principal had told the parents there was no place for her in the school, that she would have to withdraw and transfer to another school.

If you were the teacher, how would you interact with your school principal? With the child herself? With the child's parents?

If a child is excluded because of his or her race and then also reveals that he or she is gay, lesbian, or transgender, issues of identity become even more salient. The question of *intersectionality* also becomes important because if a student is both Black or Brown and gay (for example), then the marginalization or oppression may be exacerbated. Here it may be useful to ask colleagues to consider their own identity, using Taubman's categories of fictional, communal, and autobiographical identity.

Reflecting on Identity

What is your fictional identity (created by others)?

What is your communal identity (created by members of your group(s))?

What is your autobiographical identity (the ways in which you would like to be known)?

How do these identities conflict and how are they consistent?

When I think about my own identity as a White, liberal, Christian woman with a strong commitment to social justice, there are definitely elements that seem incongruous. At one point, when I was a member of a Baptist community, my church friends created for me a "fictional identity" that assumed I did not drink or play cards. Of course, on the flip side, my Baptist colleagues assumed I would support anti-abortion legislation— a policy at odds with my "liberal" political views. When I consider my "communal" identity, I am seen as a productive and committed faculty member, a staunch advocate of public education. However, none of this reflects my "autobiographical identity," which emphasizes the joy I find in hiking or sailing and other summer outdoor endeavors. For me, these conflicts are relatively minor; however, if I were a Black woman, or a Muslim, or a lesbian as well, the conflicts might be considerably more intense.

Some Possible Additional Prompts for Free Writing or for Dialogue

1. What are some assumptions people make about you based on how you look or act that you feel are incorrect?

2. What are some aspects of yourself (interests, talents, background) you feel the need to hide?

3. How do you think people would respond to you if they knew these things?
4. How would you like other people to see you?

Addressing Ability and Disability

As previously indicated, we sometimes equate ability or lack of ability with racial or social class characteristics. However, sometimes our assumptions are due to deeply rooted practices or policies that also need to be challenged. We assume, for example, that the ways we test or screen for programs to serve gifted and talented students are appropriate, and that those who are identified deserve the special attention they often receive. And, too often, we assume that it is simply a natural consequence that the predominant gifted population is White (or Asian), while it does not seem unusual for our other special education programs to be overpopulated by Black or Brown students.

Educators too often assume that students identified for placement in special education classes need to have slow, sequential (boring) educational tasks that emphasize memorization or that use flash cards that decontextualize information. However, these are truly the least helpful pedagogical approaches and delay necessary student progress; unless we accelerate the learning of those who are behind academically, they will continue to lose ground and never be able to compete on a level playing field.

The National Center for Education Statistics asserts that America's schools enroll 6.3 million "students with disabilities." In education, unfortunately, disability is generally considered within a medical model, where disability comprises a condition to be treated or cured and those who deviate from our image of those who are healthy and normal are viewed as being less than fully capable. Hence, we label children and marginalize them, thinking of needed accommodations as being onerous and expensive. Too often, if a child has some kind of identifiable "disability," we permit the disability to define them, and ignore the reality that people with disabilities may face discrimination due to pervasive and established ideas about what "normal" people can and cannot do. In these ways, schools often perpetuate the normalization of oppressive social constructions instead of challenging prevailing norms to promote equity.

What Would You Do?

Olivia was a bright, curious young lady who applied to be part of a gifted and talented program in her neighborhood high school. The criteria for acceptance into this particular program included a test of analogies and verbal reasoning—activities in which she excelled. However, when asked to write a short essay explaining why she wanted to participate in the program, her grammar and spelling errors raised concerns on the part of some teachers who argued against her admission. On further investigation, one teacher learned that Olivia had previously been identified as having a learning disability, and so asked how a child with so many challenges could ever be considered "gifted?"

Fortunately, one of the teachers who was tasked with admissions to the program understood that having an identifiable learning disability should not disqualify her for the program. Olivia excelled in high school, became a provincial champion debater, graduated with high honors from university, and is now completing doctoral studies as she works as Director of Curriculum and Instruction in the same school district where she attended high school.

What a disservice it would have been had Olivia's learning disability been used to limit her and relegate her to a vocational program with low expectations and little to challenge her!

The key here is to consider each student as a whole person, with capabilities and limitations and not to use any single characteristic as one that defines or limits the person.

An Example

I often think about a colleague who lost her ability to hear when she was two years old. She holds a PhD from a major research university and is an associate professor at another institution. My colleague signs, and travels with a hearing assist dog. Arriving at a conference where we were presenting in a symposium together, she recounted her experience at the airport. The flight attendant had pulled her aside and offered her a manual that explained security and safety procedures for those who were blind. What an insult!

Too often, because someone is experiencing one kind of challenge, we assume their capacities are impaired in other ways as well. Educators must reject this tendency and work to normalize various kinds of abilities and disabilities. At the same time, we must resist the tendency to assume that because a student has advanced knowledge or ability in one subject area, we can generalize that ability to all other subjects. Identification for gifted or talented programming must be consistent with the kinds of programming offered. No one program is likely to meet the needs of all children, or to meet all the needs of any one child.

Thus, there are numerous problems related to how we identify and think about academic ability and or disability and these must be acknowledged in addition to the others discussed here—race, sexual orientation, gender identity, religion, immigrant status, and so on—when we consider the topics covered in the following chapters—issues of public and private good, and ways to ensure that the curriculum is engaging, emancipating, democratic, and equitable for all students.

For now, it might be productive to play the "Alien Visitation Game." In other words, sit in your staffroom or in a classroom and pretend you are an alien, having just arrived on earth for the first time. A variation of the game might be to sit blindfolded, or with ear plugs, and to record simply what you can see OR hear, without the benefit of more information

Alien Visitation Game

What do you see? What do you hear?
    What seems exciting?
What seems strange?
How would you describe your visit
    when you return "home"?

Figure 2.4   Spaceship.

Who is talking and who is not?
Is there anyone who does not seem to be included? Is there a leader?

Addressing the Challenges of Newcomers

Finally, we turn to the challenges of newcomers, including transfer students, immigrants, refugees, and asylum seekers. Once again, our assumptions about each of these groups need to be unpacked and sometimes deconstructed.

For transfer students we need to know the reason for the change. Is the student transitioning from one gender to another? Has the family had to relocate for employment? Is the child simply seeking a new start? How best can we support the change? This student may simply need someone, or a small group of students, assigned to "teach them the ropes" and to show them around.

If the new students are immigrants, it is useful to know a little about the culture from which they are coming. Sometimes, in order to avoid cultural gaffs, it is also important to know the religion to which they adhere. (For a Muslim, for example, a common error is for the receiving educators to stand, walk toward the parents, and reach out to shake their hands in a welcoming gesture, forgetting that it is inappropriate for Muslim adults to touch a non-relative of the opposite sex.) If the student is also an English language learner, it is important to revisit the school's language policies. Do they permit the child to speak in his or her home language to ensure understanding, while at the same time, encouraging responses in English (or the language of instruction)? If the child must be placed in a separate program for English language learners, how can we, at the same time, ensure that he or she meets local students and can quickly become an active participant in the full academic and social life of the school? Can we provide both a "buddy" who knows their culture and language AND a local "buddy" to help with integration and social connections?

These questions are all exacerbated when we address the needs of refugees and asylum seekers who may also be undocumented. Once again, we need to remind ourselves that children do not choose their circumstances and that it is our job and commitment to teach all children to the best of our ability. And once again, this may require challenging our political and cultural assumptions. This is especially true given that xenophobia seems to be alive and well in the United States and other developed countries in the 21st century. We will need to remind ourselves and each other that, according to the *1951 United Nations Convention Relating to the Status of Refugees*, refugees are to be accorded the same rights as citizens related to education, legal assistance, and freedom of religion; they are also to receive the most favorable rights accorded to all other foreign nationals with respect to employment, property ownership, access to housing, and higher education. It is also useful to know that, despite many current political efforts to disparage and to discourage refugees, research has determined that refugees arrive in a new country with a large variety of skills and in general contribute greatly to the political and economic life of their new country. For example, Kerwin (2018) reported that

> refugees that arrived between 1987 and 1996 exceed the total US population, which consists mostly of native-born citizens, in personal income, homeownership, college education, labor force participation, self-employment, health insurance coverage, and access to a computer and the internet.

In other words, like other countries, America needs, and benefits from, immigrants who generally become loyal and contributing citizens.

An Example

There is no doubt that there are challenges for educators who strive to modify their approaches to teaching to ensure that all students can progress. How, for example, should we address the needs of a child like Gabriel?

Gabriel recalls that when he was five, he, his parents, and his four older siblings walked for weeks to escape the Sandinista regime in Nicaragua that had killed two of his uncles and confiscated his family's possessions. He remembers how tightly his father held him as they stumbled across a treacherous river to the opposite shore. He recollects his first weeks in Miami, where the family lived in a cramped one-bedroom apartment, surrounded by people who spoke a confusing language and engaged in unusual behaviors. Finally, he recalls his new school, and placement in a special education class where people did not expect much of him and the work seemed very easy.

How do we assess Gabriel's needs and what kind of placement will serve him best?

Would it make a difference if you knew that his father was an engineer in Nicaragua and that his mother had owned her own business?

How should teachers describe Gabriel and what "labels" should they not use?

Assessing Progress

How do we know we have challenged negative assumptions? This is always an important question. How can we measure or at least "assess" the changes for which we are striving? Obviously, it is difficult to assess changes in belief or attitude; however, there are certainly some indicators one can anticipate, as indicated by the examples on the following table:

Desired Change	Documentation	Still Needed
New Knowledge	Evidence of new curricular resources being used	
	Observations of people who are using information presented in new ways	
	Participation in article or book discussions	
	Sharing of articles, information	
Changed Beliefs/Attitudes	Self-reports	
	Decrease of labeling	
	Decrease of negative comments	
Changed Behavior	Challenges to negative comments	
	Better student attendance	
	Fewer student transfers	
	Fewer disciplinary incidents	

Note that the reason I have used student attendance and disciplinary incidents to help assess changes in behavior on the part of educational leaders as well as fellow students is that we stated earlier that one basic hypothesis of transformative leadership is that when students feel respected, welcomed, and included, they are more likely to attend school and to be able to concentrate on the learning activity at hand.

Depending on how transformative leaders handle and address mindsets that need to be transformed to create a more equitable climate, there will also be other indicators. For example, in Chapter 7 of *Transformative Leadership in Education* (Shields, 2016), we read about a principal named Dr. Cox who, upon hearing student reports of someone being called "terrorist" or "suicide bomber," insisted that her staff explore the situation. In turn, this resulted in an overall effort throughout the school to understand and address this issue. Regular school-wide dialogue about such challenging topics would be another excellent indicator of mindsets being changed.

Concluding Thoughts

An Example Continued

Gabriel's story ends well, but not because educators were sensitive to his needs or proactive in helping him adjust to his new situation. In fact, he was left to languish in a special education class until his tenth-grade year when he had found a job working at a local social security office and was preparing to quit school. Fortunately, in his workplace, another worker recognized his prowess and skill with computers. Upon further investigation, this colleague learned that Gabriel's teachers actually consulted him whenever they had a computer problem, but this skill somehow was not enough for teachers to question his placement in a dead-end program.

With support and encouragement from his co-worker, Gabriel finally plucked up the courage to ask his tenth-grade teacher if he could transfer to a regular class.

What Would You Do?

Both the teacher and the principal refused to transfer Gabriel. What would you have advised?

How would you have supported Gabriel?

And where do you think Gabriel is working now?

Gabriel persisted, and ultimately, after taking summer courses and additional classes at night, he was permitted to enroll in regular classes where he attained his graduation certificate. This opened doors to further education, a university degree, and an exciting career as the principal technical consultant on major construction projects, including the Trump Tower in Chicago and in New York. In fact, recently he sent his former co-worker an email from a luxury suite with a private hot tub overlooking the Caribbean where he was residing at the company's expense as he completed a major technical installation.

The point of this chapter is to remind educators that *children do not choose their circumstances*, but when we label them, or make assumptions about their ability based on unrelated factors, such as skin color or family circumstances, we are constraining them, preventing them from accomplishing all that they are capable of.

Thus, the principal and teacher described at the beginning of this chapter who believed there was nothing they could do to limit a child's free speech and stop his teasing of a classmate with a gay parent were WRONG. We can and we must do something to ensure that all students feel safe and secure, respected, and included in our schools. We must distinguish between a child's belief (which is permitted) and inappropriate and negative behavior (which can and must be corrected in a public-school situation). In this case, the child of gay parents had the same right to be in the school as children of heterosexual parents and to expect that no-one would taunt him for his family situation. This is not only inhumane but certainly undemocratic (with a small d).

It is of the utmost importance that educational leaders identify and address their implicit bias, reject deficit thinking, racism, sexism, homophobia, and xenophobia, and ensure that social class and poverty do not color our thinking. Changed beliefs are the starting point for changing policies, pedagogy, and curriculum. They undergird the introduction of culturally and linguistically relevant teaching and leading as educators begin to better understand the lived experiences of students as well as their specific needs and challenges.

All educators must be engaged in this effort to ensure that all students are given opportunities to learn and to develop fully—and even, in some circumstances, to surpass the conditions of their birth. Thus, it is essential for educators to recall the story of Gabriel and many others like him. Student success must not be due to luck but to the support and educational efforts of wise and caring teachers and leaders.

Note

1 For a thorough explication and critique of Payne's work, see Gorski, P. C. (2008), Peddling poverty for profit: Elements of oppression in Ruby Payne's framework, *Equity & Excellence in Education, 41*(1), 130–148.

References

Bertrand, M., & Mullainathan, S. (2003), Are Emily and Greg more employable than Lakisha and Jamal? A field experiment on labor market discrimination, *American Economic Review, 94*(4), 991–1013.

Gorski, P. C. (2008), Peddling poverty for profit: Elements of oppression in Ruby Payne's framework, *Equity & Excellence in Education, 41*(1), 130–148.

Johnson, H. H. (2008), Mental models and transformative learning: The key to leadership development? *Human Resource Development Quarterly, 19*(1), 85–89.

Kerwin, D. (2018), The US refugee resettlement program — A return to first principles: How refugees help to define, strengthen, and revitalize the United States, *Journal on Migration and Human Security, 6*(3), 204–224.

Kosciw, J. G., Greytak, E. A., Zongrone, A. D., Clark, C. M., & Truong, N. L. (2018), *The 2017 National School Climate Survey: The experiences of lesbian, gay, bisexual, transgender, and queer youth in our nation's schools.* New York: GLSEN.

Loewen, J. W. (2005), *Sundown towns.* New York: The New Press.

Payne, R. K. (1995), *A framework for understanding poverty.* Highlands, TX: aha! Process, Inc.

Shields, C. M. (2016), *Transformative leadership in education,* 2nd ed., New York: Routledge.

Shields, C. M., Bishop, R., & Mazawi, A. E. (2005), *Pathologizing practices: The impact of deficit thinking on education.* New York: Peter Lang.

Starratt, R. J. (1991), Building an ethical school: A theory for practice in educational leadership, *Educational Administration Quarterly, 27*(2), 185–202.

Wagstaff, L., & Fusarelli, L. (1995), Establishing, collaborative governance and leadership. In P. Reyes, J. Scribner, & A. Scribner (Eds.), (1999). *Lessons from high-performing Hispanic schools: Creating learning communities.* New York: Teachers College Press.

Wible, P. (2016), Her story went viral. But she is not the only Black doctor ignored in an airplane emergency. *The Washington Post*. accessed November 2018 at www.washingtonpost.com/national/health-science/ tamika-cross-is-not-the-only-black-doctor-ignored-in-an-airplane-eme rgency/2016/10/20/3f59ac08-9544-11e6-bc79-af1cd3d2984b_story .html.

Tenet Three
Redistributing Power in More Equitable Ways

Tenet Three of transformative leadership theory examines how we use power for good or ill and helps us to identify what needs to be changed to be more equitable.

- What kind of power do you have?
- When and how do you use it?
- When and why do you feel powerless?

These questions and those contained in boxes throughout this chapter might be the basis for some free-writing exercises, some honest dialogue, and some probing investigation. In what ways is power inequitably distributed in your organization and what might be the impact if we redistributed power more equitably?

Too often we talk disparagingly about power, as though it were a negative force, and yet, when a power source is interrupted, we recognize the importance of a consistent power supply. There is no doubt that our lives are made more difficult

> Transformative leadership does not imply the diminishing of *power*, but the diminishing of *un-democratic power relationships*.
>
> (Quantz, Rogers, & Dantley, 1991, p. 102)

when we cannot simply turn a switch to make a cup of coffee, turn on a heating or cooling system, prepare a meal, or when there is a gas shortage with long lines at the pumps.

It is therefore important for us to distinguish between power as a desirable force and one which, particularly when being used, is the source of inequity and distress for others. Many are familiar with the image of a toddler crying for solace after being separated from her parents or caregiver at the US-Mexican border in the summer of 2018 (Figure 3.1). The rules stated that no adult could touch a child, and so she stood, in tears, looking up at the legs of an adult and at the huge wheel of a truck.

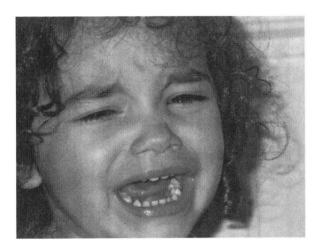

Figure 3.1   Child crying.

We do not know why the child at the right is crying (Figure 3.1), but:

- When you look at this picture what do you see?
- If you were an adult standing by, what would you do?
- If you were told not to touch her, what would you do?
- What instances can you think of in which power could be used in education to resist the rules or policies in order to provide increased equity—or even solace—to children?

Power takes many forms and thus we can exercise power *over* others, power *with* others, or power *to* accomplish a goal.

For Reflection

Give an example of each kind of power in your institution and discuss how each creates, or does not, equity for students.

Power over others …

Power with others …

Power to …

 ## Power *over* Others

In education, we exercise power *over* others when we use our power to punish, to shame, or to exclude. A good example is offered by ways in which schools exercise what are commonly called "discipline policies." The *Cambridge Advanced Learner Dictionary* defines discipline as "to teach someone to behave in a controlled way." Etymologically, discipline comes from the Latin word *discipulus*, the word for pupil, and *disciplina* (knowledge or instruction), which also relates to the word *disciple* (a follower). Discipline, therefore, teaches ways of supporting and developing students, while punishment is simply a way of "causing someone who has committed a 'crime' to suffer, by hurting them or causing them to pay." Although it is true that the earliest use of the word discipline in English was punishment-related and implied a kind of religious chastisement, it is important to reflect on whether we believe students are really "committing crimes" or whether they are simply learning to become productive and caring citizens. Thus, it is critically important to answer the following questions:

What are the goals of your [discipline] policy?

Is the policy intended to punish or to teach?

The 2014 Data Snapshot of the US Department of Education's Office for Civil Rights is available at the following site: https://ocrdata.ed.gov/Downloads/CRDC-School-Discipline-Snapshot.pdf 🔗. It would be useful to download and print copies of this Data Snapshot for all teachers in your school to provide a basis for discussion and reflection about the data. Also examine the data for your state and go to https://ocrdata.ed.gov/DataAnalysisTools /DataSetBuilder?Report=6 🕿 to find the data for your district or school. Again, use the data as a basis for dialogue or free writing.

For Reflection and Discussion

How do educators in your school explain the following facts and statistics from the Data Snapshot?

- Black students represent 16% of the student population, but 32–42% of students who are suspended or expelled.
- On average, 4.6% of White students are suspended, compared to 16.4% of Black students.
- Students with disabilities are more than twice as likely to receive one or more out-of-school suspensions as students without disabilities.
- While boys and girls each represent about half of the student population, boys receive nearly three out of four multiple out-of-school suspensions and expulsions.
- 6% of districts reported suspending out-of-school at least one *preschool* child. Racial disparities in out-of-school suspensions also start early.
- Black children represent 18% of *preschool* enrollment, but 42% of the preschool children suspended once, and 48% of the preschool children suspended more than once.

Think about it. Preschool children are being suspended; "babies" are being suspended more than once! And we know that according to a 2006 study by Gary Sweeten of Arizona State University, a first-time arrest during high school nearly doubles the odds of a student dropping out; a court appearance nearly quadruples those odds! Studies of school suspension have also typically found that 30% to 50% of those suspended once will be suspended again. Moreover, when students are suspended or expelled, they are not in the classroom learning the material that others are receiving, and hence, are falling farther and farther behind.

Because out-of-school suspensions can be dangerous, some states have developed policies forbidding them, at least for young children. In Illinois, for example, Public Act 100-0105 prohibits early care and education providers from expelling young children (ages 0–5) from their program on the basis of the child's behavior. In addition, Public Act 99-0456,13 which went into effect in September 2016, required substantive changes to school discipline practices and policies, including the elimination of any broad-based use of zero tolerance policies. In addition to other requirements, schools must make substantial efforts to consider "appropriate and available" alternatives to exclusionary discipline, ensuring that suspension, expulsion, and school transfers are a measure of last resort.

What Would You Do?

Consider the following story, told to me by a superintendent (with tears in his eyes).

> One of my most promising students was suspended and at 1:40 in the afternoon, he was shot and killed. There's no mom at home, you know. I mean he was on the street and he got shot and killed. It's not like Ozzie and Harriet. Middle of a school day. So that's why out-of-school suspension to me is just so archaic.

Would this incident prompt you to change your discipline policy or any other school policies or practices?

The foregoing is obviously dramatic, but what are the overall consequences of suspensions or expulsions? Note, of course, that school safety and the safety of all children must be preserved, but the data are clear that the majority of suspensions are for non-compliance or subjective, attitudinal issues (such as lack of respect) and not for endangering others.

The website of Teaching Tolerance at www.tolerance.org/magazine/fall-2009/pushed-out contains a number of other stories of students being punished that might also form the basis for excellent dialogue among teachers ✐. One of these follows.

For Example

Teaching Tolerance cites the story published in the *St. Petersburg Times* of a ten-year-old girl who found a small knife in her lunchbox, placed there by her mother, for cutting an apple. She immediately gave the knife to her teacher but was still expelled from school for possessing a weapon. How would you handle a similar incident?

What other examples of inappropriate use of power over others can you identify from your workplace?

Power *with* Others

One of the ways to redress the inequitable use of power is to ensure that we are working together, using power *with* others instead of exercising power *over* others. To do so, some schools, in recent years, have begun to focus on what have become known as restorative practices, or restorative justice. One principal from a school in New Zealand described her approach.

An Example

We want the kids to be internally motivated to do things. Our restorative processes that we have here are embedded across the school, so it's not just behavior management, it's around how we do things. What is the issue? What is the barrier? What's not working? Okay, let's deconstruct it a bit and let's see what we can do, then let's put it together in a way that we can do it. Everyone feels part of that. We have a restorative facilitator here. Things come to her, whether the students self-refer, "Oh, miss, I think I need to go home, because if I see her, I'm going to give her a crack." ... She will totally unpack the issue with both sides and then she will talk about, "How are we going to fix this?" first, individually, with each group, and then bring them together to facilitate fixing that. What was my part in it? What was my part to play? What did I do that made it worse? If you think about someone, for example, if someone has hurt someone else in some way, the person that's been hurt also has to think about what their part in the issue was as well. How can I stop that from happening again? Perhaps if I hadn't said that in that way, they wouldn't then have shouted that hurtful thing to me. It's really just a teaching process ... We've also done some brain understanding, because I think with restorative practices you need to understand a little bit about how the brain works and why you have those responses, and why students come in with those responses.

> The principal described how powerful the process had become, especially when used with all conflict situations whether involving students, teachers, or parents, and described the difference it had made in the school.

She said,

> I've been involved in some really powerful restorative meetings, where I've gone in thinking, "Oh, this could really be going one way or the other." In one incident with two girls, I was really worried because one mom had had a fight with another parent on the netball court a couple of months earlier. She was quite fiery. The other one was a Samoan family, so they can be quite fiery as well. In the end, these two Moms, so different people, were in tears and hugging, and the girls, "Okay, this has really worked well."

Here we see the difference between exercising power over people and helping them together to work out differences and disagreements.

In what ways is this account similar to, or different from, the ways in which discipline is handled in your schools?

Working toward Win-Win

We are all familiar with an approach to problem solving that is known as win-win. An excellent example of this may be found in the exercise called the Ugli Orange Activity that was developed by the George Mason University Institute for Conflict Analysis and Resolution Fairfax, Virginia.

In this activity, the faculty would be divided into two groups, with one being given a task assigned to Dr. Roland, and the other group a task assigned to Dr. Jones. Then one person playing Dr. Roland is paired with another playing Dr. Jones and on command, each pair begins to negotiate. The goal, in each case, is to acquire the rare Ugli orange so that each one's purpose may be fulfilled. One has the goal of preventing a deadly nerve gas attack that could kill thousands of people, while the other's goal is to cure and prevent a disease contracted by thousands of pregnant women that causes severe birth defects.

Here I will not disclose the solution to the activity, as it is important to let pairs proceed to reach a decision themselves. However, it is important to note that in this case, a win-win solution is possible, while in many instances in real life, in which the playing field is inequitable to start with, a win-win solution may simply perpetuate inequity.

Rejecting Win-Win

At one point in my career, I was told of a high school with a high Asian population that had tried to encourage more participation by the immigrant Asian parents in the governance of the school. After finding that the Asian parents seemed uncomfortable and less willing to speak in the presence of the dominant English-speaking Caucasian parent members, the decision was made to have two distinct parent groups—one Caucasian and the other Asian.

What do you think was the result?

Not surprisingly, when the Asian parent group made a recommendation that the still dominant-power Caucasian parent group disagreed with, the recommendation was discounted—and this held true whether the recommendation related to out-of-school social activities, curriculum, or parent-involvement suggestions. The response was simply that the "newcomers" were unaware of the norms and traditions of the school.

If we want to work and exercise power together, it is important to ensure that everyone holds adequate information to participate fully.

An Example

Aline was an international graduate student from Taiwan who had come, with her two school-age children, to complete graduate studies in America. She recounted that her children's school did an excellent job of translating messages and newsletters into the home languages of many of the students but indicated that she still did not feel comfortable trying to attend events such as parent-teacher meetings.

Why might Aline feel uncomfortable?
What additional information might she need?

For Aline, the issue was not that she failed to know there was a meeting scheduled. It was simply that a translation was not enough. For someone from a different tradition, it would have been helpful to offer further explanation. What happens in a parent-teacher meeting? What are the expectations? How should she dress? What should she bring? Will she have to speak? What if she doesn't know something she is asked? Should the children come too? How long will it last?

Without this information, one can easily see why it would seem safer, less intimidating, and more comfortable for parents like Aline to simply stay home. If we truly want to exercise power *with* others, we must provide them with enough information so they feel comfortable offering ideas and participating in new processes and activities. Hearing their perspectives will enlighten all of us.

Power *to* ...

Power to refers to the unique potential of every person to shape his or her life and world and of groups of people to exercise their collective capacity to fulfill their goals. To exercise "power to" first requires that educators reflect on the goals of education. What are we working toward? Why are we doing what we are doing? Ultimately, three broad goals have generally been recognized: a custodial function, an individual one, and a collective one. How do you define each one? For discussion of these goals, see pp. 63–67 in *Transformative Leadership in Education* (Shields, 2016) or download the questionnaire called "The Goals of Education" from the eResources.

The Goals of Education

How do you define each one?

The custodial goal of education is to

_____

_____

The individual goal of education is to

_____

_____.

The collective goal of education is to

_____

_____

Here, when we are considering the concept of *power to,* it is important to consider all three goals together. We must draw on the individual skills, talents, and commitments of each person within the organization and unite them as collective action in order to make significant change.

Political scientist Robert Putnam asks the important question of why some societies and governments succeed while others do not. His response is a surprisingly simple one. He analyzed numerous tales of collective action—action intended to promote safety, security, and stability as people work together to accomplish a goal. He reports that, "What best predicted good government ... was choral societies, soccer clubs, and cooperatives." In other words, societies characterized by networks of civic associations and "an active culture of civic engagement," flourished.

> The root of social trust was civic engagement.
>
> (Putnam, 2001, p. 29)

An Example

Putnam tells the story of a neighborhood near San Jose, Costa Rica, in which, some time earlier, the founder of a neighborhood organization had introduced El Ley del Saludo (the law of the greeting). When the association was formed, everyone agreed to leave for work five minutes early to have time to say "Hello" to each neighbor. The result was that norms of friendship and solidarity developed, crime declined, and problems were quickly solved. Almost everyone bought a referee's whistle to warn of danger or potential thievery; they took up a collection to buy a siren and set up a phone network. The result was that robberies declined from approximately two a week to roughly one a year, and the neighborhood gained a reputation for tranquility and solidarity.

What are the lessons from this story?

Power to is the beginning of trust as well as the source of social action that may result in overcoming inequitable situations. Martin Luther King (1963), in his famous *Letter from Birmingham Jail*, wrote: "Freedom is never voluntarily given by the oppressor; it must be demanded by the oppressed." It is unfortunate that those who have the most power and privilege must often be convinced by collective action, including protests, sit-ins, and demonstrations, that their privilege is causing others to experience hardship, marginalization, and oppression. However, the power of working together to challenge and change inequities cannot be overestimated.

Congressman John Lewis, known for his persistent civil rights work and tireless efforts to gain voting rights for all, offers another inspiring example of someone who motivates others to take risks for socially just causes and who stands up for what he believes—despite the fact that he has been beaten and close to death on several occasions for his stance. A further example of people banding together to accomplish a goal is the Women's March in Washington that expanded in 2017 to mobilize more than four million people calling for gender equity worldwide. Although much work remains to be done, the fact that the march continues annually and that in November 2018 more women than ever before were elected to congress, including the first Muslim woman, the first Native American congresswomen, and the first bi-sexual senator, is indicative of the collective power unleashed by the movement.

What other examples can you think of in which collective action has led to more equity?

a) _____

b) _____

c) _____

d) _____

e) _____

As you reflect on your own educational organization and identify where change is needed, it is important to take time to build some support for a shared vision. Consider the following questions.

For Reflection

What do we want to accomplish in our school?
Who can we mobilize to help us?
How can we garner support?

Assessing Progress

How do you know if you have reduced the inequitable use of power in your organization? What measures might you use? Here test scores will be of little use, although parent or student surveys that ask about satisfaction or participation might be useful.

Other ways of assessing progress might be to identify

- The number of parents who attend school functions compared to previous years
- The number of people from minoritized groups with whom you have had conversations about their hopes and goals for their child and for the school
- The number of students who participate in clubs and other school activities, including leadership activities
- The number of community partnerships the school has developed and added to your "community map" (described in Chapter 1)
- The actual changes that have been made in terms of suspension or expulsion rates
- New programs and activities that include diverse groups of people, and not simply the wealthiest or most powerful

Concluding Thoughts

It is important not to lose hope because it is rare to be able to convince everyone in the organization. But it is important to find some others who share your vision, who will work with you, and support your attempts at change. As a starting point, you might want to find a few others to "pilot" a new idea, recognizing that, as Michael Fullan (1993) argues, "Belief follows action" and that when others see the positive impact of a change, it will garner additional support. You cannot wait to have everyone on board but might want to send up a "trial balloon," to ensure that you have at least a small group of people willing to act together as you move forward. Once others see your success and enthusiasm, it becomes easier to persuade them to join the effort.

As Plato stated, so many centuries ago: The measure of a man is what he does with power.

What are you doing with your power?

> Participation fosters a sense of collective identity as people discover shared interests around which they might act jointly.
>
> (Quantz et al., 1991).

 ## References

Fullan, M. (1993), *Change forces, Probing the depths of educational reform*. New York: Routledge Falmer.

King, M. L. (1963), Letter from Birmingham Jail, Facing History and Ourselves. accessed June 2019 at www.facinghistory.org/resource-library/letter-birmingham-jail.

Putnam, R. D. (2001), What makes democracy work? In S. J. Goodlad (Ed.), *The last best hope*. San Francisco, CA: Jossey-Bass. pp. 25–32.

Quantz, R. A., Rogers, J. & Dantley, M. (1991), Rethinking transformative leadership: Toward democratic reform of schools. *Journal of Education*, *173*(3), 96–118.

Shields, C. M. (2016), *Transformative leadership in education*, 2nd ed., New York: Routledge.

Sweeten, G. (2006), Who will graduate? Disruption of high school education by arrest and court involvement. *Justice Quarterly, 23*(4), 462–480.

Tenet Four
Balancing Public and Private Good

Tenet Four of transformative leadership theory argues the need to balance the goods of education in order to empha-size both individual and collective benefit, in other words, both public and private good.

This chapter discusses the difficulties and challenges related to the need to balance individual growth and development (private good) with preparing students to participate collectively in civil society (public good). To do so involves a reconsideration of policy and pedagogy in which we ensure students are taught to think both critically and creatively.

There is little doubt that education is both a powerful force for societal improvement and a source of assistance and support to individuals. Schools, colleges, and universities all proclaim the individual benefits of education in an attempt to improve and maintain student enrollment. In fact, as we saw in *Transformative Leadership in Education* (Shields, 2016) and in the last chapter, since the beginning of formal education, there have been debates about the appropriate nature and goals of schooling. Should formal education be grounded in values and beliefs about a better society or should it simply aim to promote individual development, job training, and career opportunities?

Some would argue that the purpose of education and therefore of leadership is to promote individual growth; others would argue it is to socialize participants into an existing society and social order; still others would argue its over-riding function is to prepare students for citizenship, and in particular for democratic citizenship. Transformative leadership theory recognizes the importance of balancing all of these goals but is cognizant that a focus on social change is sometimes neglected. Yet it is necessary for all citizens to participate in, and experience fully, the possibilities offered by a deeply democratic and mutually beneficial society. In some ways, this balance is reflected in the following quote by Astin and Astin:

> We believe that the value ends of leadership should be to enhance equity, social justice, and the quality of life; to expand access and opportunity; to encourage respect for difference and diversity; to strengthen democracy, civic life, and civic responsibility; and to promote cultural enrichment, creative expression, intellectual honesty, the advancement of knowledge, and personal freedom coupled with responsibility.
>
> (2000, p.11)

The Private Goods of Schooling

Given the current focus on what is sometimes known as "college and career readiness," this tenet requires significant change in the ways in which we have come to think about the goals and purposes of education. A recent publication from the US Department of Education sets forth the expectation that funding will be tied to "state-developed standards in English language arts and mathematics that build toward college and career readiness by the time students graduate from high school" (USDE, 2010, p. 2). The booklet includes a section entitled "Why focus on college and career readiness?" in which the discussion explains that too many students have to enroll in remedial courses in college and that too many employers report that students are ill-prepared for the workforce when they graduate from high school. Despite the truth of these statements, a balanced focus on collective good is missing. Nowhere in the publication does one find reference to "society," "democracy," or "public good."

This is consistent with historian David Labaree's (1997) argument that education's emphasis has changed from a focus on preparing citizens to one in which education has become a commodity. He writes that education has:

> increasingly come to be perceived as a private good that is harnessed to the pursuit of personal advantage; and, on the

whole, the consequences of this for both school and society have been profoundly negative.

(p. 43)

In private good, education is seen as a means of acquiring a credential, a way of securing a better position, and as a "proving ground" for a market ideal rather than as a means of acquiring knowledge or of citizenship training. Success or failure are thus attributed solely to an individual's effort and achievement with no thought given to barriers or supports offered by social structures or educational institutions. Nevertheless, it is rare that success or failure may be solely attributed to one's individual effort or actions, despite the fact that policies for schools too often imply that this is the case.

It is important to acknowledge that the private goods of education are essential, as no parent wants his or her children to grow up without the skills to hold a job and become independent and self-supporting citizens. To that end, we often identify the goods of education in terms of possible lifetime earnings or annual income, as indicated in Figure 4.1.

Although these estimates are most often presented in an attempt to convince students to remain in school and to progress to the next level, I have heard of students seeing this chart and wanting to seek the immediate

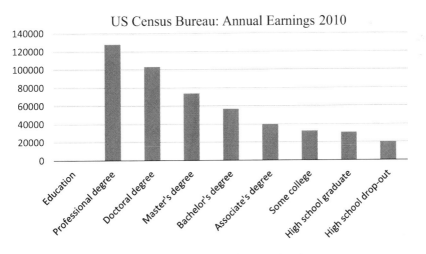

Figure 4.1   Estimated annual earnings by education level.

gratification to be realized by dropping out of school and earning $20,000. Here again, the activity from Tenet Two "Could You Live on the Minimum Wage?" might inform the discussion.

It is also important to note that there are strong correlations between health, happiness, and levels of education in that there is evidence that educated individuals tend to live longer lives than their uneducated counterparts, have lower rates of suicide, much lower levels of incarceration (65% of those incarcerated have not completed high school), and even lower rates of divorce. These are benefits that cannot and should not be discounted both for their individual impact and because society as a whole benefits from an educated citizenry.

Nevertheless, we also know that making a successful test score the measure of an educated citizen is pure folly, as many standardized tests do little more than evaluate an individual's ability to memorize or to guess at the right pre-answered question. In fact, school policies that require specific test scores as a pre-requisite for elective courses or for participation in extracurricular activities may be counterproductive in that it may well be participation in one of these activities that could motivate improved academic performance as well. The pressure placed on some individual students to make parents or teachers proud has also been associated with increased anxiety and stress.

Moreover, when a whole subgroup of children (perhaps English language learners [ELL] or African American) is reported as not having attained the expected grade-level standard, consider the shame perpetrated on the whole group for "letting down" the school or for being responsible for the school receiving a failing grade.

It thus behooves educators to carefully examine their policies and practices to determine which, if any, are placing undue importance on individual attainment or behavior, failing to acknowledge the collective, societal influences that are relevant to student performance and behavior.

One activity that can help teachers understand the relationship of societal advantage to test-taking ability is to engage in an examination of some practice questions for the Miller Analogies test (often used for graduate school admission). Although this is a test that purports to assess reasoning ability, it is highly culturally embedded. Several questions included on recent practice tests are:

Hemingway : _____ :: Woolf : Thackeray

A. Fitzgerald
B. Homer
C. Garcia Marquez
D. Waugh

To answer this question correctly, one would have to know that both Hemingway and Woolf were American while both Waugh and Thackery were British. It is not simply a matter of reasoning.

Try this one:

(_____) : Puccini :: sculpture : opera

A. Cellini
B. Rembrandt
C. Wagner
D. Petrarch

Again, to answer correctly, one would not only have to know that Puccini wrote operas but also that Cellini was a sculptor.

These examples begin to demonstrate the culturally embedded nature of knowledge and some of the problems inherent in acting as though success or failure may be solely, or even primarily, attributed to an individual's effort without giving thought to their inherent cultural advantage or disadvantage.

Surprisingly, however, we often fail to consider similar factors when developing policy.

Discipline Policies as Examples

In this section, we examine the ways in which policies, and for the purpose of illustration, discipline policies, may emphasize private factors to the exclusion of public influences. In the previous chapter, you were invited to consider the goal of your discipline policies and to determine whether they were more punitive or more educative. To further this consideration related to public and private good, you might engage in some role-playing activities (see the full *Discipline Role Play Activity*).

Role Playing Family Influences on Discipline Policies

First, divide your teachers into three groups and ask them to role play the interactions of the family depicted on their card. Listen to the differences in the language and approaches of the three families as they interact.

Following the first round of role play, assign new roles to four teachers. One would be asked to play the role of Kevin, one of five children living with his parents (father a construction worker and mother a waitress) in a subsidized housing project. Another would play the role of Melanie, daughter of a Christian pastor who regularly attends church and Sunday School on Sunday mornings and Wednesday evenings. A third would play the role of Elliott, a child recently diagnosed with Tourette's syndrome. The fourth will play the role of the person in charge of discipline within the school.

What Would You Do?

The task is to role play the disciplinarian speaking to each child who has been sent to him (or her) because of swearing during class.

Consider:

Why did each child swear?
What should the appropriate action be?

It should become quickly apparent that no matter how hard Kevin tries to curtail his behavior, and even though he has immediately apologized for swearing, it will be more difficult for him to conform to the rules than Melanie because he lives in an environment in which cursing may be commonplace. Moreover, Elliott has a medical diagnosis and hence it may seem more legitimate to modify the policy for him than for Kevin.

No matter how important it is to create a pleasant and safe learning environment in the school, it should become apparent that the lived experiences of each child affect his or her behavior and that it is not likely appropriate to impose a similar penalty on each. Nevertheless, this is exactly what too many school behavior policies and positive behavior enforcement systems do.

Here it should also have become apparent that simply attributing individual motives to a child's behavior ignores the very real societal influences that contribute to behavior. Consider Trevon's story.

What Would You Do?

Trevon is a thirteen-year-old boy who says he is gay and has talked about having a "boyfriend." In the halls and in gym class, he has been teased and harassed by fellow students, but for the most part, he has not retaliated. One day, after being called some particularly heinous names and being shoved by one of the other boys, he threw a punch. Subsequently he was called to the office and given a three-day suspension.

Is this treatment fair?
How could it have been handled?

Why should Trevon be punished for fighting while the wider issues of teasing or even "gay bashing" are ignored? The issue here is that although there are definitely individual and private good benefits to education, much of what happens in schools relates to what also occurs in the wider society and, conversely, is preparation for students to live together as productive and caring citizens. For that reason, it is important to pay explicit attention to the public good goals and aspects of schooling.

The Intersection of Private and Public Goods

According to the Organization for Economic Cooperation and Development (OECD, 2013), educated people are more actively involved in various societal activities such as "voting, volunteering, political interest and interpersonal trust." Each of these activities, in turn, helps to contribute to the good of the whole. Moreover, an educated society experiences more economic growth and stability as well as more of the intangibles such as greater fulfillment and meaningful lives. Each of these benefits depends on the notion of public good, defined by Labaree in 1997 as a good "where benefits are enjoyed by all the members of the community, whether or not they actually contributed to the production of this good" (p. 51). These include healthcare, policing and security provisions, adequate food and housing for all citizens, and so forth. One measure of the public good is when we, as fellow citizens, are able to feel pleasure when others succeed and pain when others fail. Some benefits of this nature are provided by a progressive rather than a regressive tax, in other words, a tax that takes a larger percentage from high-income earners, in opposition to a regressive tax that is applied uniformly, taking a larger percentage of income from low-income earners.

Yet, because of Western individualism, these benefits are endangered if we do not focus on both teaching about, and preparing students for, citizenship. Indeed, as previously noted, the simplistic definition of a democracy as a system in which each person has one vote is inadequate. Almost 200 years ago, de Tocqueville, writing about his experiences with democracy in America, identified the potential for misuse of democracy, saying:

> If ever the free institutions of America are destroyed, that event may be attributed to the unlimited authority of the majority, which may at some future time urge the minorities to desperation, and oblige them to have recourse to physical force.

It is therefore critically important to help students understand the importance of using their votes to promote the mutual benefit of all. To do so requires that we also take seriously de Tocqueville's observation that he knew of "no country in which there is so little independence of mind and real freedom of discussion as in America."

> I know of no country in which there is so little independence of mind and real freedom of discussion as in America.
>
> (Alexis de Tocqueville, 1845)

The question therefore becomes, how do we teach independence of mind and freedom of discussion? And it is here that individual and collective benefits merge. And here, one of the first steps is to overcome the tyranny of test-taking and test preparation and to ensure students are being taught both creative and critical thinking.

Thinking Critically

I recall one day during the final exam period of the high school where I was teaching, two ninth-grade girls coming to me, saying

> We are so glad your exam and that of Mr. G is over! They are the thinking exams and the rest are easy.

Needless to say, Mr. G and I took great pride in that assessment and began to inform our students directly that our teacher-made exams would always be "thinking exams." One way we did this was to teach our students the six levels of Bloom's taxonomy. We informed them that they would be expected to answer questions at all levels and taught them how to use each by ensuring that our day-to-day activities and assignments required a range of skills. In fact, as a check on my own approach, I kept a copy of this taxonomy, with appropriate verbs, questions, and activities, taped to my desk. (See Table 4.1 here and in the eResources where you will find a copy to download for your own use.)

If I were teaching a unit about a novel, for one unit, I might emphasize *analysis* by asking students to classify the characters based on a physical or mental characteristic, to solve a problem, to compare several ideas, and so forth. To emphasize *synthesis*, I have, on occasion, asked students to create a game based on a novel or short story, and then to *evaluate* the game based on criteria they developed together.

Table 4.1 Bloom's Taxonomy: A Pedagogical Aid

Level	Definition	Verbs	Questions	Activities
Knowledge	Student recalls information in the approximate form in which it was learned.	Define, describe, identify, list, match, name …	Who, what, when, where, how …?	Label a diagram, fill in the blank, find answers on a page, etc.
Comprehension	Student translates, comprehends, or interprets what has been recalled.	Convert, defend, distinguish, estimate, explain, generalize, express, rewrite reorganize …	Can you explain … in your own words? What is the main idea …?	Create a report, write a letter about …, make a poster, present the information in a new way e.g., graphs, tables, etc. …
Application	Student selects, transfers, and uses data to complete a problem or task.	Compute, demonstrate, operate, show, use, solve	How is … an example of? How is … related to …? Why is … significant?	Create a webpage, build something, illustrate something, make a mural, create some rules, …
Analysis	Student breaks the information down to its constituent tasks, identifies the parts of the argument, etc.	Distinguish, diagram, outline, relate, discriminate, subdivide, compare & contrast …	What are the parts or features of …? Classify … according to …? How does … compare/ contrast with …? What evidence can you find for …? Solve problems …	Debate, diagram, ask some questions, write a business memo or a political brief for a boss with all pertinent info listed, …

Synthesis	Student originates, integrates, and combines information into a "big picture" whole—perhaps a proposal, product, or plan that is new to him or her.	Combine, compose, create, design, rearrange ...	What would you predict/infer from ...? What ideas can you add to ...? How would you design a new ...? What might happen if you combined ... with ...? What solutions would you suggest for ...?	Design something, make a game, construct a model, plan something (e.g., a trip), write a proposal for a new ...
Evaluation	Student appraises, assesses, or critiques on the basis of specific standards or criteria.	Appraise, criticize, compare, support, conclude ...	Do you agree that ...? What do you think about ...? How would you decide about ...? What criteria would you use to decide ...? On what basis do you prioritize ... in this way? What is the most important?	Hold a mock court, develop a brief for ..., a presentation to a government about a desired option, develop criteria and judge submissions (reports, stories, arguments, etc. ...)

Promoting Critical Thinking

Examine the chart summarizing Bloom's taxonomy and identify the levels at which you require students to work.

Are any levels missing?
What do you emphasize?
How could you add activities to cover the other areas?

The key to teaching critical thinking is to avoid activities that focus on memorization or simple description. In other words, if students can simply find the answer in the text, they are not learning to think critically.

Given the current increase of "fake news," and the proliferation of many types and sources of information, critical thinking is particularly important, so that students learn to distinguish fact from fiction, to understand what constitutes "truth," and to critique and consider multiple perspectives. In fact, in 2012, Giroux argued that "public education may offer one of the last spaces for true democratic thought and dialogue."

One 2016 study found that 75% of American adults who viewed a fake news headline viewed the story as accurate. Moreover, fake news can have real consequences as the following incidents clearly demonstrated:

- A man entered a pizza parlor and fired a gun at employees believing the fake news that the restaurant was a front for a child sex abuse ring.
- Almost a million people read and accepted a story that asserted that Pope Francis had endorsed Donald Trump for president.
- Almost 14 million viewers of Facebook watched and believed a totally fake video of a plane, struggling in a huge storm, doing a 360-degree flip before safely landing and letting out terrified passengers.
- Another totally false story stated that one day after the legalization of marijuana, Canada had made so much money in tax revenue from the sale of legal weed that they were able to pay off the country's entire $650 billion debt.
- A story that described a woman from Baker county Idaho being arrested and sentenced to prison for breastfeeding continues to circulate despite its falsehood.

To help us distinguish fake news from "truth," it may be useful to use the short YouTube video by Damon Brown, *How to Choose Your News,* 🔗 as a basis for discussion. Similarly, the following questions are intended as a guide for critically examining newscasts.

Identifying Fake News

How do we know? Check the facts. What would you check first?

Check the name of the "offender" in a list of court reports.

Check the name of the Idaho County – and you will find that it does not exist.

Try to follow other information in the story.

Try to find other instances of the same incident being reported.

What else might you do?

To protect democracy, educators cannot afford to close their eyes to the threats to democracy or to inclusive, informed, civic participation that occur on an almost daily basis from multiple sources.

Thinking Creatively

To be productive citizens, it is also important for students to learn to think creatively. Here, numerous other enjoyable activities can be used and a model, such as Lucas' Five Dimension Model, 🔗 may be useful. It summarizes activities that may be used to help students generate new ideas and to "think outside the box" by emphasizing persistence, collaboration, discipline, imagination, and inquisitiveness.

For example, asking students to think about all the uses for soap, or to brainstorm ways to improve an e-reader, or anything related to your curriculum, might be fun ways to introduce a new topic. In science, I might ask students to brainstorm how water becomes polluted or in math, to explain uses of algebra in everyday life, and so on.

The key is to ask students to generate new ideas regardless of how impractical they may seem, in order to stimulate imaginative thinking. Moreover, as the model indicates, to think creatively requires persistence, discipline, imagination, inquisitiveness, as well as collaboration.

Using Collaborative Games

Teachers are well aware of the many websites that offer ideas for numerous age-appropriate cooperative games. In addition, the activities on Lucas' model that promote collaboration lead directly into the kinds of thinking that promote public good. Here, Lucas lists cooperating appropriately, giving and receiving feedback, and sharing the product.

To supplement that repertoire, I advocate using a puzzle called simply "Broken Squares" (see 𝒫). In this puzzle, participants are divided into groups of five, with each person being given three differently shaped puzzle pieces with which he/she is asked to make a perfect square. No talking is permitted, although, in order for the group to complete the goal of each person completing a square of the same size, there will need to be collaboration and sharing of puzzle pieces. The catch is that unless everyone is aware of what others need, one or two will be unable to complete their square, while the others may sit smugly having completed "their" square, without realizing that the whole group needs to adopt a different solution to have five squares of similar sizes. Debriefing this activity can also provide useful practice in the free discussion advocated by de Tocqueville.

Moving toward the Public Good

The final aspect of emphasizing public good to be discussed here is ensuring that all policies and practices of the school are focused on building the capacity of both teachers and students to ensure equity of opportunity for all. This is particularly important given the obvious inequities in our wider society and the unfortunate debate over whether we truly are "our brother's keeper."

The Stanford Center on Poverty and Inequality 𝒫 provides an excellent summary, with charts and tables, of inequity in American society, although it is essential to acknowledge that similar inequities occur in other developed countries.

Before you look at the Stanford data, list the inequities in your own city or country and determine what your students should know about them.

Data about Inequity

Among other inequities listed by the Stanford Center, one learns that

- Over the past 30 years, wage inequality has increased substantially.
- The average CEO compensation in 2009 was 185 times more than the wages of the average production worker.
- On an average night in America, there are more than 750,000 homeless people, with disproportionate numbers of males, Blacks, veterans, and disabled people.
- Approximately 1.4 million children experience homelessness in a given year in the United States.
- Although the pay gap between women and men has narrowed over the years, in general women still earn only 80% of what men receive for the same or similar work. (African American and other minoritized women earn even less.)
- The child poverty rate in the United States is 21%, higher than in Scandinavia, Britain, Canada, and considerably higher than the 13% rate that comprises the average of the 34 OECD countries.
- There has been a tremendous increase in incarceration rates in the United States in the past half century, giving the United States one of the highest rates in the world. Particularly alarming is that 37%—in other words, one third of young Black male high-school dropouts—were in prison or jail in 2011.

Look around.

Can you imagine one third of your students in jail?

What can you do to ensure this does not occur?

Dialogue about Equality and Equity

In order to promote dialogue about balancing individual and collective rights, it may be useful to spend some time discussing the implications of the following well-known image of children standing on boxes (Figure 4.2). (For this and other related images, search for "children on boxes democracy image.")

Figure 4.2   Children on boxes.

You may be surprised to learn that sometimes when I ask a school staff member to discuss these images, the discussion about equity is met with considerable opposition. Some argue that every child has a right to an equitable education and taking the box from the child on the left is unfair. Indeed, they argue, he/she needs resources too. And of course, they are right. Nevertheless, if one child needs eyeglasses and others do not, we do not allocate glasses to everyone. If one child needs a hearing aid to be able to understand the teacher, we do not require all children to wear hearing aids. In other words, we can and should allocate resources according to need.

For Reflection

What is the impact of allocating resources or support equally?
What are the implications of moving the box from the child on the left to the one on the right?
What is represented by the third image?
What would be the implications if the fence were also removed?

In this case, it is the goal that should determine what supports should be offered. No matter how hard the child on the right may try, he/she will not be able to grow longer legs to enable him to see over the fence. Yet, here, seeing the game is the goal, while in the classroom, optimal learning for all children is the goal. And although the child on the left can still see the game when he has a box, it does not really help him to see any better.

Some argue that the right-hand image, sometimes called "democracy," requires the removal of the fence altogether and although in some instances that may be true, here, if the goal is safety, then the fence is likely essential. You may also find it interesting to note that in one quite cynical variation of this image, the third image is labeled "reality" and has the child on the left standing on six boxes, the middle one, standing on one box, and the one on the right standing in a hole in the ground absolutely unable to see anything through or beyond the fence. In another also cynical variation, a new higher fence has been erected in front of the "equity" image; this new right-hand image is labeled "capitalism" and has the subheading "pay for your tickets freeloaders."

The point here is that it is important to develop a shared understanding among teachers about the goals of the school and the best ways to attain them, demonstrating the importance of both individual and collective good, and thinking about ways to promote each. To do so, it is important to identify the skills each person in the organization has, what skills and abilities need to be developed, and what supports and resources are needed to help everyone competently attain these goals.

Building Capacity for Democratic Citizenship

Capacity building is the process by which individuals and organizations obtain, improve, and retain the skills, knowledge, tools, equipment, and other resources needed to do their jobs competently or to a higher level.

What skills do you need to build for yourself?
What skills do you need to promote among your students?

Once the necessary skills for civic engagement and participation, for the solidarity identified by Putnam in the previous chapter, have been identified, it is critical to reflect on how to proceed. Social scientists have identified three core principles that may be used to achieve collective or public good: dominance, reciprocity, and identity (or identification). *Dominance* is associated with the (often inappropriate) use of power discussed in the previous chapter. The ways in which *dominance* operates may be complex, with hegemony, threats, or force being possible applications. A *reciprocity* principle rewards those who are perceived to be contributing to the group benefit and punishes those who pursue self-interest at the expense of the group. The *identity* principle emphasizes the identity of participants as members of a community. Let us reflect on a simple school problem and how these principles may play out.

What Would You Do?

Each year, your whole school community ends the year with an excursion that is intended to be both educational and enjoyable. Last year, the decision was to hire a bus and head to Disney World. Those who were able to participate had a wonderful time, but some who could not afford the trip remained behind. Hence, although many want to repeat the trip, there has been discussion of taking an overnight camping trip to a nearby National Park in order to include more people.

Using the *dominance* principle, to ensure that everyone can participate, the principal unilaterally decided that this year the trip will be to the park. Once he identified the overall cost of the trip, he determined that 80% of the participants could cover the cost of everyone, so even those who could not afford it could participate freely. The repercussions of using this principle too often are obvious in that although it provides an equitable solution, there is a risk of oppression as people's voices are not heard and their opinions disregarded. There will also likely be backlash by those who do not want to be told they must pay extra to support those who cannot pay.

If the *reciprocity* principle is considered, those who resist supporting others would be "punished" by the group for pursuing their self-interest at the expense of others. In this case, if a few wealthier parents refuse to pay more than the cost to cover their child, they may be reprimanded or even ostracized for their self-interest. On the other hand, they may spark conflict and a revolution that may even result in the trip being canceled.

The solution based on the *identity* principle lies in the full participation and deliberation of all participants as members of a community. Here, a group deliberation in which everyone is concerned about the ability of all to participate could result in a similar decision, but with everyone knowing that their voices have been heard and the decision has been taken by all for the good of the "community." At the same time, anyone who happened to disagree might still be critiqued and outcast.

To help build capacity to contribute to the collective good, game theory in which participants can practice with such activities as the prisoner's dilemma, a mixed interest game, or burden sharing may be useful. One possibility is a classroom version of a public good game that can be played with a deck of playing cards. A link for complete instructions is included here. 🔗 This game uses a regular deck of playing cards and asks participants to engage in a series of moves in which they play a number of cards. Players earn $4 × the number of red cards kept by the student plus $1 × the number of red cards played by all. Ultimately the game demonstrates that when participants work together in the common interest rather than simply to amass points for themselves, everyone benefits. The point of all of these games is to demonstrate that contributing to the public good, in the long run, offers greater benefits than action that apparently enhances self-interest.

Sometimes educators are reluctant to engage in the dialogue and activities intended to promote increased awareness of inequity, responsibility, or public good, arguing that young children especially cannot handle these issues and should not be burdened with them. To attempt to disprove this argument and to support both the need and the ability of students to engage in controversial issues, I present the following dialogue shared by a colleague who wanted to determine how well young children understood the concepts of "we" and "they" (see Pillsbury & Shields, 1999).

We and They

My colleague wanted to determine whether conscious discussion about self and others could be productive in fostering student reflection and growth, and so asked a class of first-graders, "Is it wrong to call a bunch of people 'they?'" During the conversation, one student asked, "What if someone said, 'We're playing by ourselves?'"

After two intervening statements, a little girl reflected, "Umm, like, we're playing by ourselves so you can't play."

> As they explored this issue, a boy said softly, almost to himself, "Oh no, don't say that you can't play."
>
> Shortly thereafter, another boy asked, "But how are you going to describe someone else without saying 'they'"?
>
> Therein lies the problem, clearly delineated by first-graders.
>
> A girl continued, "When you say 'they,' it's like … 'they' is different and whenever we say 'we' it's not different."

This example of a conversation in which the use of language was explicitly explored with first-graders suggests that such an activity holds considerable potential for heightening awareness and raising sensitivity on the part of students, even among those who are very young. As these children began to recognize, it is not that the use of "we" or "they" is inherently right or wrong; rather, it is how a comment is framed and what sense of self or other is being represented that is important.

Engaging students, even as young as first-graders, in dialogue about what comprises "we" in terms of promoting public rather than simply private good may be both productive and extremely enlightening. However, as with previous tenets, the assessment of progress is difficult and often elusive.

Assessing Progress

Once again, although measuring progress on standardized tests may indicate individual growth in learning, it is not adequate in and of itself. Other measures might include a collective examination of teacher-made tests and the extent to which they promote various levels of thinking on Bloom's taxonomy as well as the extent to which these teacher-made tests seem to be free of bias related to socioeconomic status or ethnicity. Other indicators of progress might be:

- Evidence of differentiated disciplinary enforcement for different children
- More dialogues related to the influence of community factors on behavior
- A reduction of blame for individual infractions or lack of progress

- An increase in the number of teachers collaborating on lessons or activities
- An examination of lesson plans over a one-week period to identify creative thinking exercises
- An examination of lesson plans to identify collaborative activities
- Identification of levels of critical thinking required to succeed on teacher-made tests.

Concluding Thoughts

When de Tocqueville visited America and wrote his seminal volumes in which he both described and critiqued our form of democracy, he made several particularly damning comments. The first was that "In democratic society each citizen is habitually busy with the contemplation of a very petty

> The advantage of democracy is not, as has been sometimes asserted, that it protects the interests of the whole community, but simply that it protects those of the majority.
>
> Alexis de Tocqueville

object, which is himself." Although one might take exception with the characterization of the self as being petty, it is critically important for educators not to promote individual interest at the expense of preparing students to participate fully in civil society. If we fail in our mission to balance public and private good, the result may well be the anarchy de Tocqueville described that results from the tyranny of the majority over the minorities.

The protection of the interests of the majority is not the advantage advocated by transformative leaders and transformative leadership theory, which is based on respect, justice, and equity for all. For that reason, balancing public and private good in school practices and policies is one aspect of promoting a more just and inclusive organization.

References

Astin, A. W., & Astin, H. S. (2000), *Leadership reconsidered: Engaging higher education in social change*. Battle Creek, MI: Kellogg Foundation.

accessed December 2006 at www.wkkf.org/knowledge-center/resou rces/2007/01/Leadership-Reconsidered-Engaging-Higher-Education-In -Social-Change.aspx.

de Tocqueville, A. (1845/2012), *Democracy in America*, Tr. H. C. Mansfield. Chicago, IL: University of Chicago Press.

Giroux, H. A. (2012), Can democratic education survive in a neoliberal society? *Truthout*. accessed April 2019 at https://truthout.org/articles/ can-democratic-education-survive-in-a-neoliberal-society/.

Labaree, D. F. (1997), Public goods, private goods: The American struggle over educational goals, *American Educational Research Journal, 34*(1), 39–81.

Organization for Economic Cooperation and Development (OECD, 2013), Education indicators in focus. accessed June 2019 at https://ww w.oecd.org/education/skills-beyond-school/EDIF%202013--N°10%20 (eng)--v9%20FINAL%20bis.pdf.

Pillsbury, G., & Shields, C. M. (1999), Shared journeys and border crossings: When "they "becomes "we," *Journal for a Just and Caring Education, 5*(4), 410–429.

Shields, C. M. (2016), *Transformative leadership in education*, 2nd ed., New York: Routledge.

USDE. (2010), College- and career-ready students. accessed May 2019 at www2.ed.gov/policy/elsec/leg/blueprint/college-career-ready.pdf.

Tenet Five
A Focus on Democracy, Emancipation, Equity, and Justice

Tenet Five of transformative leadership theory focuses not only on ensuring that our educational institutions eliminate all forms of discrimination and oppression, but that we teach about the continuing prejudice, oppression, and subjugation that persist throughout our world.

Given the rapid movement of peoples throughout the world, it is important for all educators to be aware of some of the reasons for suffering, displacement, refugee status, and immigration in order to be able to better serve students from areas of conflict and trauma, as well as to inform others about these situations worldwide. Because these and other examples of inequity need to be addressed in public schools, Tenet Five argues for a focus on democracy, emancipation, equity, and justice. Combined, the values of Tenet Five comprise a sense of "freedom."

Democracy, as we have seen, requires an understanding of both individual rights and also the collective or public good and acknowledges that we may need to contribute to goods from which we do not ourselves benefit. This ensures that the nation is organized to provide maximum and mutual benefit for all, rather than simply rewarding those who begin with the most advantages.

Emancipation reminds us that, despite the end of legal slavery, not everyone is equally free. Marginalization and oppression, including child and sex trafficking, forced labor, and indentured servitude, are still widespread as are oppressive circumstances that are not necessarily physical.

Equity is distinguished from equality (as the image of children on boxes trying to see the baseball game demonstrated) in that it does not imply treating everyone in the same way with the same supports and resources; rather equity requires acknowledging that because everyone does not start from the same place, or have the same needs, it is not fair to treat them in exactly the same way.

Justice implies a combination of equality, fairness, access, and human rights. It is sometimes thought to apply more to legal principles, although there is also widespread recognition of commutative (justice in transactions), distributive (justice in the distribution of material goods), and social (justice in social and cultural opportunities and situations) justice as well.

In 1995, Kincheloe and Steinberg talked about the importance of telling compelling stories about our lives as educators and of formulating answers to pressing educational questions and challenges. To do so, they asserted, requires that our systems of meaning must be "just, optimistic, empathetic, and democratic" (p. 2).

An Example

In some jurisdictions, policy related to overnight field trips has taken the needs of transgender students into account. The policy states that an administrator or counselor might ask a transgender student to identify other students with whom he or she feels comfortable sharing a room. If a student is a minor, the policy also requires seeking written permission from the parent of the transgender child to share the identity information with the other parents.

This policy seems to me to represent the kind of education suggested in 1995 by Kincheloe and Steinberg, education that is just, democratic, empathic, and optimistic. It is *just* in that all children have the opportunity to participate in the field trip; it is *empathic* because it shows understanding of gender identity issues; it is *optimistic* in that it assumes other parents will also support the transgender child's participation, and it is *democratic* in that it promotes the good of all. But not everyone is necessarily on the same page.

For Reflection

What would you do if the parent of the cisgender (non-transgender) child refused to permit the sleeping arrangement?

How is the education you are offering in your school

Just
Democratic
Empathic
Optimistic?

In what ways is the education you are offering *not* just, democratic, empathic, or optimistic?

How can you change it?

 ## Thinking about Democracy

As previously indicated, there are many simplistic ways of thinking about democracy. However, here I present several more complex and complete ways of thinking about democracy.

Criteria for Democracy

In 1956, Robert Dahl identified five criteria for assessing democracy. These were:

1. Voting equality—in which everyone has a vote and knows each vote will be counted fairly and equally.
2. Effective participation—in which there are no barriers to voting or other public activity and in which everyone has the ability and opportunity to participate.
3. Enlightened understanding—in which people have the opportunity to freely make choices about what is best for them (as in which academic program one should choose rather than being funneled into one based on assumptions and identity markers).

4. Control of the agenda—here in addition to voting, everyone should have an equal opportunity for input and feedback in some way.

5. Inclusion—the democratic process must be available to every human being, in other words, to all teachers, parents, and students in the school.

How well is your school doing at implementing each of these?

Although these criteria provide extremely useful starting points, other theorists have re-examined these principles and provided additional ways of thinking about democracy.

Deliberative Democracy

Woods (2005) posited that the role of democratic leadership was to share *power* (by dispersing leadership and diminishing hierarchy), share *hope* (by extending opportunities to realize humanistic potential), and share the *fruits of society* (through fair distribution of resources and cultural respect)" (p. 139). To accomplish these goals, he argued the need for what he called "deliberative democracy"—a form of democracy that promotes civic engagement through thoughtful, informed discussion and deliberation.

For Reflection

How are you sharing

Power

Hope

The fruits of society?

In 2012, Giroux posited the importance of public education, arguing that "schools should be viewed as crucial to any viable notion of democracy, while the pedagogical practices they employ should be consistent with the ideal of the good society." Adopting the principles of either Woods or Dahl, or both, helps to create the kinds of spaces Giroux was calling for, spaces that include the need for enlightened or informed understanding and civic participation.

 ## Reflecting on the Need for Emancipation

Here I use the term emancipation instead of the more common word "liberation" to emphasize the heinous nature of many current oppressive practices. We often think of emancipation in relation to the dreadful American history of slavery and particularly as it pertains to Lincoln's "Emancipation Proclamation" of 1862 in which he decreed that "all persons held as slaves within any State or designated part of a State" would be "thence forward, and forever free." The slave trade, which is often traced in the United States to the arrival on a Dutch ship of twenty Africans in Jamestown, Virginia, was a horrendous part of American history, not in the least because it comprised the *legal* ownership of one person by another, and played a valuable role in the economic development of the nation. Berry (2017) describes this period of slavery as one in which people

> were bought and sold just like we sell cars and cattle today. They were gifted, deeded and mortgaged the same way we sell houses today. They were itemized and insured the same way we manage our assets and protect our valuables.

Moreover, it was legal for individuals and states to codify these attitudes as embraced by the Texas Ordinance of Secession, adopted by the Secession Convention on February 1, 1861, by a vote of 166 to 8:

> We hold as undeniable truths that the governments of the various States, and of the confederacy itself, were established exclusively by the white race, for themselves and their poster- ity; that the African race had no agency in their establishment; that they were rightfully held and regarded as an inferior and dependent race, and in that condition only could their exist- ence in this country be rendered beneficial or tolerable.
>
> (Texas Ordinance, 1861)

Modern Day Oppression and Slavery

If slavery and oppression had ended, as Lincoln might have hoped, with the Emancipation Proclamation, there would be no need to use the term emancipation here or to consider ways in which people are still treated as chattel and personal possessions. However, unfortunately this is not the case.

Today an estimated 40.3 million people worldwide are in conditions of what is generally known as "modern slavery," as they are exploited and controlled by others in forms of human trafficking, forced labor, child labor, enforced child marriage, and other activities. The difference, of course, is that these activities are no longer legal. Nevertheless, modern "slavery" exists in every country in large numbers. Hence, emancipation today emphasizes the "fact or process of being set free from legal, social, or political restrictions" (Figure 5.1).

> Start by identifying as many instances as you can from recent news reports of people who needed to be set free.

Figure 5.1   Breaking chains.

What instances did you recall? Did you think of the

- Nearly 80 people who were found near Laredo, Texas, crammed into the back of a truck trying to enter the United States without proper documents
- Estimated 300,000 children who serve as child soldiers, some younger than ten years old
- 72 million children who are in hazardous work that directly endangers their health, safety, and moral development (recall that not all child labor is considered to be slavery)
- 11% of women worldwide who were married before reaching the age of 15
- 17,500 people who are trafficked into the US annually, 81% for sexual purposes
- 10, 615 people who, in 2017, contacted the National Human Trafficking hotline?

Who are the Victims?

In most cases, victims are enticed by promises of a better life, improved living conditions, clothes and food, and someone to take care of them.

An Example

Graciela explains that when she was ten years old, her parents died in a car crash. She slept on the streets until she met a woman who took her home, promising to look after her. But instead, she made her do the housework until, when she was 15, she was given to a different family as a domestic worker. On her first day, she was raped and beaten by a man who said that if she did not do as he asked, he would continue to beat her. Instead, she was forced to have sex with many different men each day, until one day, she finally escaped.

Another Example

Emma's experience began differently.

One day, while at the mall, Emma, a pretty sixteen-year-old, met a man who started taking her out and buying her clothes and meals. Not long afterwards, he convinced her that if she would work for him, she would never have to rely on anyone again and that she would have everything she needed. At seventeen, she was forced to earn at least $1000 a day as a sex worker and if she didn't, the trafficker threatened her family who lived nearby.

Although the majority of children trafficked are girls, boys suffer too. Consider those who are forced to work as farm laborers or in other menial tasks as reported in 2018 in the *Trafficking in Persons Report* by the US Department of State. They also provide the example of Raul (p. 7).

An Example

When Raul was in high school in the Dominican Republic, he jumped at the opportunity to go to the United States to continue his education. A family friend offered to be his sponsor and hire Raul in his restaurant while Raul attended school. Shortly after Raul arrived in the United States and began attending the local high school, his sponsor pulled him out of classes and forced him to work in his restaurant full-time for less than $1 an hour. The sponsor withheld Raul's passport, threatened him, and sexually abused him. Raul was forced to live in filthy conditions in the restaurant. After an anonymous call to the national hotline, law enforcement officials raided the restaurant and arrested Raul's sponsor.

The Role of Educators

These stories are dramatic. They reflect the need for true emancipation today—the need to set these children "free from legal, social, or political restrictions." So the question is: What can educators do?

1. First, educators need to be on the look-out for children who may be in dire circumstances, change their habits, and eventually drop out of school. Some children who come into our schools as refugees, having escaped abysmal circumstances in their countries, will have experienced similar situations.
2. It is important to understand that many students come from situations in which they have been traumatized. Refugee students who come from war-torn countries as well as many students who live in areas in which there may be violence due to drugs or gangs may have witnessed vicious acts, suffered the brutal death of a loved one, or simply been distressed due to fear of such violence.
3. At the same time, very few educators will have to teach students whose situations are, or have been, as dire as those described previously. So, it is necessary for us to reflect, once again, on which students in our schools are oppressed or marginalized by attitudes, practices, and policies that constrain them. Although schools do, in some ways, "hold" children against their will in that schooling is mandatory in most countries until a certain age, within that policy there are ways of adding additional constraints and penalties for some students. It is to these we now turn our attention.

For Reflection

How can we ensure that our school and classroom practices are inclusive, democratic, and socially just?

How can we promote equitable opportunities and outcomes for all students?

Can you identify any students who may have been traumatized?

What do we want students to know about ways in which others are not free?

Promoting Equity

The unintended consequences of many school policies and practices are inequitable outcomes for different groups of students. We have previously seen how policies related to disciplinary infractions often negatively affect Black and Brown students and contribute to the school-to-prison pipeline. The differential outcomes of these policies contribute directly to the need for liberation or emancipation and for rethinking our policies and practices. Here again, free writing, pair-share conversations, open dialogue, and role play may be useful as you consider the following questions.

> What are some other restrictive aspects of schooling that relate to legal, social, or political decisions or arrangements?
> What policies are not democratic?
> What cultural assumptions restrict participation?
> What social practices inequitably control students?
> What pedagogical practices are undemocratic?

It is estimated that from one half to two thirds of all school-age children experience trauma—defined as a negative external event or series of events that surpass a child's coping skills. Policies that may result in inequitable, unintended consequences may exacerbate the impact of trauma. Thus, it is increasingly important for educators to understand the nature of trauma, and to learn how to address it in the classroom. Such traumatic experiences may include maltreatment, witnessing or experiencing violence, serious illness, having an alcoholic or incarcerated parent, homelessness, or the loss of a loved one. Traumatic experiences can impact brain development and behavior inside and outside of the classroom.

A 2015 account by McInerney and McKlindon from the *Education Law Society*, reports that

> In one representative sample of children in western North Carolina, 68% of 16-year-olds had experienced trauma and 37% had experienced two or more traumatic events. More specifically: 25% had been exposed to violence. 15% had

experienced the violent death of a sibling or peer. 7% had experienced physical abuse by a relative. 11% had experienced sexual trauma in the form of sexual abuse, rape, or coercion. 33% had experienced another injury or trauma (e.g., serious accident, natural disaster).

(p. 2)

Although these statistics seem almost unbelievable, they are regularly repeated throughout the United States, with children in urban areas experiencing even higher levels of trauma. In fact, instead of talking about many students as having experienced post-traumatic stress disorder (PTSD), some scholars and experts have begun to think of them as suffering from *chronic* PTSD in that they may have faced repeated situations of trauma. Thus, having educators trained in some of the principles of trauma-informed education (as introduced briefly in the next paragraph) will bring considerable understanding about how these students should be treated. This training includes discussion of how trauma may affect the intellectual development and functioning of children as well as strategies related to mindfulness (mindful listening and mindful bodies), conflict resolution, restorative questioning, making I-statements, and more.

Note: The full McInerney and McKlindon article outlines principles of trauma-informed learning and provides case studies to assist with teachers' understanding.

An Example

I recall, when teaching high school some years ago, I discovered that a quiet, well-behaved female student had written obscenities all over the school-owned, assigned textbook. I was appalled and surprised. Mona had given no indication in class that she was unhappy or that anything was wrong.

How would you handle the situation?

When a child is acting out or behaving inappropriately, the *Education Law Center* recommends that teachers learn to ask appropriate questions and to respond accordingly. Their 2015 report argues that at the heart of trauma-based approaches is the belief that

> students' actions are a direct result of their experiences, and when students act out or disengage, the question we should ask is not "what's wrong with you," but rather "what happened to you?" By being sensitive to students' past and current experiences with trauma, educators can break the cycle of trauma, prevent re-traumatization, and engage a child in learning and finding success in school.
>
> (McInerney & McKlindon, p.2)

If we are aware of some implications of children having experienced trauma, we will be more likely to address misbehavior appropriately and equitably. We will know that instead of punishing inappropriate behavior, it may be more productive to ask questions to better understand their behavior. Research tells us that these children may:

- Find it challenging to pay attention and process new information
- Develop sensory processing difficulties that can contribute to problems with writing and reading
- Have difficulty responding to social cues and may withdraw from social situations or bully others
- Be distrustful of teachers in that authority figures have failed to provide safety for them in the past

Many school policy handbooks include lists of behavior considered inappropriate that include such offenses as: bullying, harassment, defacement of school property, disorderly conduct, failure to serve detention, profanity toward staff, and so forth. And although it is critically important to the security and safety of all students to ensure a safe and orderly learning environment, all infractions of these (and other rules) may not be equal, and hence should not necessarily receive similar responses.

It is important to ask at every turn:
What has happened to this child and how should I respond?

An Example Continued

Although I am not at all sure I understood the trauma-informed principles, or that I responded appropriately when I discovered Mona's infraction, I did call her in and talked quietly to her. I learned that her vulgarities were a cry for help and took steps to get to know more about her. As I did so, she began to focus more and to perform well in class. Ultimately, as I was moving to a new city at the end of the school year, she asked if she could come to my house, help me organize and pack. As we talked, she apologized for her actions and asked how she could make restitution.

Four keys to teaching students who have experienced some form of trauma include:

- Avoid power battles
- Always treat others with "absolute regard"
- Maintain high expectations
- Be a positive role model.

I think about a ninth grade class I taught some years ago in which several students had quite severe behavior problems. Remember context is important and zero tolerance rules were not in place, nor were concerns about school safety as pronounced as they are now (in that school shootings such as Columbine and Parkville had not occurred).

Two Examples

One boy regularly came into the classroom and called me "Mom." His attention-seeking behaviors were significant and on one occasion, he moved to the back of the room and lay across several desks.

On another occasion, a tall, male student who liked to consider himself "tough" actually took out a switchblade at his desk and quietly used it to sharpen his pencil.

What would you have done?

I am quite sure that today, more than 40 years later, I could not simply ignore either behavior, but at the time that is what I did. I did not want to get involved in a battle of wills, nor did I want to give either of them any more attention than the behavior warranted, so I ignored both, although I did make eye contact with them to ensure they knew I had seen them. And you may not be surprised to learn that when neither behavior brought a desired outcry from me, the teacher, the behavior was quickly terminated by each student, without me having to interrupt the class in any way. Obviously, I learned quite a lot about behavior from these students given that these incidents are still vivid in my memory. Intuitively, I had implemented the four keys identified previously.

Ensuring Justice

Justice, sometimes defined as "fairness in the ways people are dealt with," is a basic requisite of schooling. Moreover, educators are quite familiar

> Injustice anywhere is a threat to justice everywhere.
>
> (Martin Luther King, Jr.)

with the perspective of Martin Luther King, Jr. that injustice anywhere is a threat to justice everywhere, and hence, it is important to reflect on the ways in which justice and injustice, access and opportunity play out in our schools.

Only as transformative leaders identify democracy, emancipation, and equity as bedrock principles for the operation of their schools will they be able to claim they are operating a "just" school. Only as we ensure that all students have equitable access to high-quality programs and that all are held to high expectations and standards can we consider that our schools are just. Only as we fully include students whose home language is different from the language of instruction, who may be physically or intellectually challenged in some way, who may look or dress differently from the norm can we claim that our schools are just. If we believe that some children, because of the color of their skin, the origin of their parents, the conditions in which they live, are less able to learn, less deserving of our attention and resources, then our schools are not just.

In some cases, as we have seen previously, it is implicit bias, based on pervasive and often implicit cultural assumptions that perpetuate inequitable policies and practices and inhibit justice. In many cases, these assumptions may be referred to as *essentializing*. This concept implies that different ethnic, social, or cultural groups have essential *characteristics* that are intrinsic to that group. In some cases, the assumptions pertain to all or most students and include beliefs such as: "If they don't want to learn, that's their problem, not mine" or "I have students who do their work, and they shouldn't be shortchanged by those who don't."

These assumptions are dangerous because they are often based on perceptions related to appearance, parents' employment, or the behavior of older siblings. In addition, they fail to acknowledge that what students learn, and whether they are motivated to learn, depends to a large extent on what and how the teacher teaches. Saying, "I taught it; they just didn't learn it," is akin to a car salesman saying, "I sold it; they just didn't buy it."

Other assumptions relate more particularly to children from minoritized families (often Black or Brown) who live in challenging economic situations. These include assumptions such as: "You have to be mean and very tough with them because that's all they know" or "These poor students need a great deal of structure and direct instruction because they have so little structure at home." Sometimes, we hear people state that there is a culture of poverty that requires children to reject what they know from home in other to be successful. Again, this is a negative, deficit-oriented, essentializing mode of thinking that bears no resemblance to the positive attitudes that undergird transformative leadership.

For schools to be just, students do need various kinds of role models, all of whom need to be able to communicate caring and high expectations. Moreover, although a certain amount of structure is necessary, too much structure stifles creative and critical thinking and prevents initiative and innovation. Students do not need to all respond to the same writing prompts, to all be at a certain place in a given lesson at the same time, reading the same text, and responding like parrots to pre-ordained ideas about what the lesson is about. Moreover, no just system of schooling would encourage students to reject their own family in order to enjoy academic or career success.

Inclusive Practices that Promote Democracy, Emancipation, Equity, and Justice

Consider Jason's story and appeal to teachers.

An Example

My grandparents came to America from Taiwan when they were teenagers. They actually met here and moved to Michigan to work in the auto industry. No, they did not open a restaurant. Among their many friends are people who are Black, Mexican, and White. My parents are also second-generation American and speak English perfectly. My Mother is a teacher and my father is a social worker. I want to study philosophy and ultimately to become a professor. Why does everyone expect me to be good at math? It is my least-favorite subject. And while I am at it, why do people always ask me where I am from? I am American.

For Reflection and Dialogue:

Identify the assumptions in Jason's story.
Watch the short YouTube video *Where are you from?* &
Share your impressions.
Can you identify a time when you asked an inappropriate question?

Ultimately, it is important for teachers whose cultures or backgrounds differ from those of many of their students to

- Show all students they care for them as individuals.
- Show them that they expect them to succeed academically.
- Show a desire to learn something about their cultures, histories, languages.
- Remember they are individuals who cannot (and should not be asked to) speak for their sociocultural group.

On occasion, news media report stories of students who seem to have been inappropriately punished or who have been excluded from various school activities. A few anecdotes are included here to prompt discussion about how to overcome practices that are inequitable and do not promote justice. On each occasion, these reports could provide the impetus for a brief, whole staff discussion to better understand how educators perpetrate inequity.

1. Approximately 40% of gay or lesbian students report having been "put off" team sports by earlier negative experiences at school. Other reports indicate that some school leaders have banned "gay-straight alliances," or have prohibited gay students from taking a same-sex partner to a school prom or other event. In 2018, Humm reported that

   > A middle school in Stafford County, Virginia, had a lockdown drills that students do to prepare for an active shooter. The students all went to their respective boys' and girls' locker rooms, but staff couldn't decide where a transgender girl should go, so she was kept out of both—left in a hallway with a teacher.

2. In Australia, a report by Philip Ruddock's government commission recommended that religious schools should have the right to ban gay students based on their sexual orientation or gender identity. In the Australian state of New South Wales, all private schools have the right to discriminate against students, and in Queensland, for instance, the law allows students to be excluded or expelled if they don't follow the religion of the school, but not for being gay.

3. Another example of marginalization related to a first-grader who was not allowed to read a story from *The Beginner's Bible* for an assignment in which students were asked to read their favorite stories aloud in class.

4. In 2016, an eleven-year-old Somali refugee student was told by a teacher: "I can't wait until Trump is elected. He's going to deport all you Muslims." The teacher exclaimed, according to the American Civil Liberties Union (ACLU) letter of complaint, "Muslims shouldn't be given visas. They'll probably take away your visa and deport you. You're going to be the next terrorist, I bet." Moreover, when the boy's mother complained to the school, administrators encouraged him to withdraw (Ochieng, 2017).

For Reflection

How would you and your school handle each of these situations?
What policies might need to be revisited and what could be put in place?
With whom should you, as transformative leader, talk and what should you say or ask?

The point of these stories is to remind educators that discrimination occurs in many forms and always needs to be taken seriously. In each of these cases, students experienced repression, marginalization, a degree of dehumanization, and lack of respect; yet in many of these cases, it was educators who perpetrated the behavior that was upheld by higher courts.

The bottom line for Tenet Five is that it must play out in classroom practice in order for all students to feel welcome, included, and respected. Here educators need to understand that, despite the pressure of standards and standardized tests, their pedagogical practices need to involve all students and provide opportunities for students to bring the totality of their lived experiences to make sense of the classroom experience.

Opening the Curricular Space

Consider the following student in a sixth-grade classroom. (Note in the *Identity Activity* there are descriptions of four other children that may also form the basis for dialogue.)

What Would You Do?

Your name is Denny. You are twelve years old and are beginning to wonder who you really are. You were adopted when you were three by a single White gay man. You have been told that your natural father is Black and your Mother a Latina immigrant from Mexico. Nothing at school seems to connect with your background and you do not see the relevance of what you are learning. All you really want to do is play video games on your phone.

As Denny's Language Arts teacher, what can you do to help him learn?
What if you were his social studies teacher?
His math teacher?
His science teacher?

Curriculum as Conversation

One of the important principles of democratic education is that it should help students understand how the world works, who they are, and to determine their place in the world. A useful starting point is Madeleine Grumet's concept of curriculum, also discussed in *Transformative Leadership in Education* (Shields, 2016). Grumet decries how she watched students sitting in a classroom answering questions about black holes as though they were simply potholes. Given the recent breakthrough in our knowledge about black holes through science's ability to finally develop an amazing photograph of a black hole, her comment seems particularly salient. Grumet argues that

> when we say that we are educating someone, we are introducing that person, young or old, to ways of being and acting in the world that are new to his or her experience. ... Education is about a human being making sense of her life in the world ... What is basic is not a certain set of texts, or principles or algorithms, but the conversation that makes sense of these things. Curriculum ... is the process of making sense with a group of people of the systems that shape and organize the world that we can think about together.
>
> (p. 19)

The teachers' role is a difficult and challenging one in which they are supposed to help students make sense of their world, address the prescribed standards, and also prepare them to pass requisite tests. In addition, expert teachers ensure they use the five pedagogical principles identified in Figure 5.2.

> Curriculum ... is the process of making sense with a group of people of the systems that shape ... the world.
>
> (Madeline Grumet, 1995)

Using these principles and what we know about students, how can we ensure each child can make the sense-making connections advocated by Grumet? How, for example, can the unique situations of Denny and others be safeguarded in a way that emphasizes democracy, emancipation, equity, and justice while, at the same time, the needs of all of children are addressed?

For the purposes of argument, let's stipulate that in the sixth grade in his state, Denny is supposed to read a novel, and learn about character development; in writing, he is to learn about figurative language and punctuation; in social studies, one of the standards is to understand the development of an industrial, urban, and global United States; in mathematics, students are to learn about ratios and proportion, percentages, and fractions; and in science, one of the major topics is to learn about designing scientific experiments as well as to develop an understanding of matter and mass.

Principle 1. Ensure that students are not spending the majority of their time sitting and listening to the teacher or copying notes from the board. Instead, they must be actively trying to make sense of the material, discussing it, manipulating it, using different thinking skills to explore the content.

Principle 2. Provide students with choices that help them accomplish Principal 1.

Principle 3. Understanding is more important than "coverage."

Principle 4. Understanding comes from talking and teaching as much as it does from being quiet.

Principle 5. Make use of teachable moments.

Figure 5.2   Some important democratic pedagogical principles.

Take time to reflect on how each subject teacher could begin to make their class more relevant.
How did you decide you could encourage Denny's learning?

The English language arts teacher could provide a selection of readings that dealt with adoption, mixed race children, and immigration, letting Denny choose from among them. The writing assignments might permit him to compare his life with the main character from the book he has chosen and also require that he use at least ten different adjectives, four figures of speech, and at least four different punctuation marks correctly in his essay.

Note: No teacher can understand all the important aspects of all the backgrounds and cultures of students in their classrooms. No-one is expecting teachers to teach about each culture. But it is important for teachers to create space for each student to be able to relate his or her own perspective to the intellectual material under consideration. Hence, creating choice that includes various aspects of the different cultures represented in a classroom is one way to provide culturally relevant instruction. Although this assignment is not necessarily different for any of the students in the class, the ability to make choices based on their unique identities and backgrounds permits both engagement and sense-making.

The social studies teacher might first have to provide some whole-group instruction to help students understand the time period being discussed and to identify some of the major changes that occurred in the development of an industrial, urban, and global United States. However, once students have mastered the general concepts, each could be asked to choose from a list of ethnic groups to further study their role in the industrialization or globalization of the United States. Here Denny would be free to choose the German-Caucasian ethnicity of his adoptive father, the contributions of Mexican immigrants, or of the African American community, again helping him to understand how to make sense of his place in the world.

Note: I am not in any way suggesting that the prescribed curriculum should not be taught, but simply that each student has the opportunity to make sense of its relevance to his or her lived experiences.

Sometimes we think that it is easiest for the language arts or social studies teachers to make their curricula relevant, and on a day-to-day basis, this may be generally true. However, if each teacher determined that for each major unit, they would include one project or homework assignment that would offer some student choice, the overall impact of this decision would be tremendous. Each year, in as many as eight subjects, the student would have a chance to select a topic of interest and to begin to make sense of the world in a more relevant way.

The math teacher could determine that an assignment based on immigration or on the ethnic breakdown of the country or state could help students to understand ratios and to engage in the calculations that would convert ratios to percentages and fractions of the overall population. (If teachers were coordinating and discussing their units among themselves, the math teacher might actually confine the inquiry regarding population growth to the period of industrialization being studied in social studies.)

The science teacher might also, after teaching the basic concepts of mass and matter and ensuring students could complete the required calculations, ask them to develop presentations related to the import or export of various raw materials used in goods that were developed during a period of industrialization and to calculate the costs of transportation based on mass or volume, and so forth. In other words, what materials were required for Henry Ford's car, how were they transported, and at what cost? Or if a later period were being studied, the calculation might pertain to components of computers as they were first developed compared to those of today, and so on, and perhaps to profit margins.

And what might any of these teachers do if a given student, perhaps even Denny, suddenly said something like, "My Dad likes to cook, and he says that copper pots are better than steel or aluminum ones for making pudding. Is that true?" Although for the language arts and social studies teachers, the comment may seem truly off the wall, it should likely not be ignored. "What made you think of that" or "how does that relate to the character you are writing about" might be legitimate responses. For the math and science teacher, further exploration of the characteristics of these metals, their relative weight, or conductivity, and so on, could validate the student's comment.

The discussion of Tenet Two of transformative leadership theory included consideration of the role identity plays in feeling secure or threatened in organizations. It is also rel-

> How others see us becomes in part how we see ourselves.
> (Henry Giroux, 1998)

evant when we consider inclusive and socially just pedagogy. The more of ourselves or our families we feel the need to hide, the more threatened we feel and the less we can focus on the task at hand. Conversely, the more we feel accepted, the more we can concentrate, as we are free to be ourselves. However, as we have seen in the foregoing discussion, unless students find themselves reflected in the curriculum and in the identities of the personnel of the school, they may have difficulty knowing who they are. In 1998, Giroux posited that "how others see us becomes in part how we see ourselves" (p. 15). Thus, how teachers think about and "see" students becomes internalized in a particularly pervasive way. (Recall how teachers' perceptions affected Sophie in *Transformative Leadership in Education*, Shields, 2016.)

Educators must constantly reflect on the messages we are communicating to our students if we are to provide a socially just and inclusive education for them, rather than keeping them trapped in inappropriate essentialized, fictional identities. The following questions may again be useful for small group dialogue, free writing, or even role play:

For Reflection

- What is our image of success?
- Is this the same image all of our students and families have?
- How does constructing newcomers as "rapists" or "terrorists" affect their sense of self?
- Is it appropriate to think of other human beings as "illegal"?
- How does our situation at birth affect our life chances, including who we can marry, where we can live, and so forth?

 ## Assessing Progress

To assess progress toward ensuring democracy, emancipation, equity, and justice will require multiple measures and methods of evaluation. If, as others have posited, student academic achievement improves the more they feel respected, secure, and engaged in the learning environment, one measure of the success of this tenet, over time, should certainly be improved student academic performance, especially on the part of those individuals who formerly seemed disengaged and unmotivated. However, this change will not happen overnight as teachers first need to become familiar and comfortable with new teaching strategies and with school policies that are not universally applied to every student in the same way. Other measures that could indicate progress toward this goal should include:

- An improvement in student attendance, as teachers attend to students' home situations, including experiences of trauma
- Changes in school policies that account for students' lived experiences
- Increased teacher discussion about students' backgrounds and needs
- Increased activities including choice and hands-on sense-making in lesson plans
- Improved ability on the part of teachers to identify inequities
- Increased sense of energy in the school as students are more fully engaged in sense-making activities.

Concluding Thoughts

Democracy, emancipation, equity, and justice are not the words that one generally associates, at first glance, with schools and educational institutions. In fact, more often, the first words that come to mind are accountability, organization, and standards.

The questions that must be asked, by transformative educators who are concerned about offering excellent and equitable education to all, are:

> Accountability for what?
> Organization of what? For what?
> Whose standards and why?

Too often, when we think about accountability, we think about it in terms of the appropriate and ethical use of fiscal resources or of adequate progress as measured by student performance on standardized tests. But we live in a democracy, founded, as the *Declaration of Independence* states, on truths assumed to "be self-evident, that all men are created equal, that they are endowed by their Creator with certain unalienable rights, that among these are life, liberty and the pursuit of happiness."

It is to these principles all transformative educators must be accountable. Nothing else will sustain our democratic society. Moreover, if we fail, we may well fall into the situation anticipated by de Tocqueville almost two centuries ago. As we saw in the previous chapter, he wrote that if the free institutions of America were destroyed, because of the "unlimited authority of the majority … Anarchy will then be the result, but it will have been brought about by despotism" (1845).

The despotism of hegemony, of causing people to feel inferior or unwelcome or of treating anyone with less than absolute regard, must be addressed for the good of all students in our schools.

 ## References

Berry, D. R. (2017), American slavery: Separating fact from myth, The Conversation, June 19. accessed January 2019 at https://theconversation.com/american-slavery-separating-fact-from-myth-79620.

Dahl, R. A. (1956), *A preface to democratic theory*. Chicago: University of Chicago.

de Tocqueville, A. (1845/2012), *Democracy in America*, Tr. H. C. Mansfield. Chicago, IL: University of Chicago Press.

Giroux, H. A. (1998), *Channel surfing, racism, the media, and the destruction of today's' youth*. New York: St. Martin's Press.

Grumet, M. R. (1995), The curriculum: What are the basics and are we teaching them? In J. L. Kincheloe, & S. R. Steinberg (Eds.), *Thirteen questions* (2nd ed.). (pp. 15–21). New York: Peter Lang.

Humm, A. (2018), Trans student excluded during shelter drill, *Gay City News*. accessed February 2019 at www.gaycitynews.nyc/.

Kincheloe, J. L., & Steinberg, S. R. (1995), Introduction: The more questions we ask, the more questions we ask, In Kincheloe, J. L., & S. R. Steinberg (Eds.), *Thirteen questions*. New York: Peter Lang.

McInerney, M., & McKlindon, A. (2015), Unlocking the door to learning: Trauma-informed classrooms & transformational schools, *Education Law Society*. accessed February 2019 at www.elc-pa.org/wp-content/uploads/2015/06/Trauma-Informed-in-Schools-Classrooms-FINAL-December2014-2.pdf.

Ochieng, A. (2017), Muslim schoolchildren bullied by fellow students, NPR, March 29. accessed February 2019 at www.npr.org/sections/codeswitch/2017/03/29/515451746/muslim-schoolchildren-bullied-by-fellow-students-and-teachers.

Shields, C. M. (2016), *Transformative leadership in education*, 2nd ed. New York: Routledge.

Texas Ordinance of Secession. (1861), Lone Star Junction. accessed April 2019 at www.lsjunction.com/docs/secesson.htm.

Trafficking in Persons Report. (2018), US Department of State. accessed April 2019 at www.state.gov/j/tip/rls/tiprpt/.

Woods, P. A. (2005), *Democratic leadership in education*. London: Paul Chapman Publishing.

Tenet Six

Interconnectedness, Interdependence, and Global Awareness

Tenet six of transformative leadership theory emphasizes our interconnectedness in a global community and thus, that we are, to some extent, "our brothers' keepers"—members of a huge, interdependent family.

The focus in the previous chapter on democracy, emancipation, equity, and justice primarily emphasized situations and circumstances related to the school and the members of its community (parents, students, educators, and community members). As we have seen, schools are shaped by the experiences and backgrounds of their students and their families. However, to be truly transformative, it is important to acknowledge that we are not only members of a local community, but of a global one as well. As Hames-Garcia asserted, "The whole self is constituted by the mutual interaction and relation of its parts to one another" (2000, p. 103). And this is true whether we are talking about how parts of the physical body affect the overall health of the body, or how various sectors of a city affect the well-being of the whole city, or whether we are thinking of the global community in its entirety.

Here the first task is to make educators aware of our interconnectedness and interdependence, and then to consider how we promote global awareness and curiosity among students as well. We cannot afford to take the position of the principal of a large high school located in a university town with students and faculty from all over the world, who once stated, "I do not have a passport. I have no desire to travel outside of this country. We have everything we need here."

How would you respond to her?

 ## Interconnectedness

Interconnectedness occurs on several levels: individual and collective, local and global, present as well as historical. At the root of all interconnectedness is relationships. Human beings are born out of relationships and live their lives in relationship to others. We have long known, for example, the importance of human touch for health and well-being. From the monkey studies in which baby monkeys favored warm, cloth-covered surrogate "mothers," to research in orphanages that studied the fate of babies who were left on their own in cribs or who were held and coddled while being fed, we have learned the importance of interconnection. They key is to determine what kinds of relationships we want to engage in, and to promote those that create health and well-being both on an individual and an international level.

I recall once taking a class held in a large gymnasium full of people. And although I do not recall the professor's name or anything else about the class, and I am sure that the instructor never knew my name, I do recall him saying that it was important to know one thing about each student's life outside of school.

For Reflection

Think about your students. Name them.
What do you know about each of them?
What are their skills, interests, and activities outside of school?
How can you learn more?
How can this knowledge help you to develop a more inclusive learning environment?

Sometimes in order to begin to get to know our students, we can administer a brief interest inventory at the beginning of the year. At other times, we can begin to know them, as I did with Mona from the last chapter by asking students to write daily or weekly journals in which you pose writing prompts that can help you better understand them.

In chapter 5 of *Transformative Leadership in Education* (Shields, 2016), you find the story of Aaron, a young student whom I believed was misplaced in my remedial English language arts class. Somehow, I learned that he was passionate about Kung Fu and particularly intrigued by Bruce Lee. Had I not taken the time to ask him about his hobby on occasion as he entered or left my class, I would never have learned how he compared Bruce Lee to great men from history and mythology such as Alexander the Great, Genghis Khan, Houdini, and so forth. And, if I had not learned about his passion, I could never have recommended that he be more appropriately placed, not in a remedial class, but in one that could support his interests and abilities.

Similarly, if Gabriel (from Chapter 2) had not encountered a co-worker who recognized his abilities and encouraged him to stay in school, and ultimately to go on to higher education, he might not ever have realized his capacity to build complicated communication networks in high-tech environments.

Relationships do not happen by accident. They take work, sometimes hard work. But it is critically important that every student has some positive role models and adults in whom they can confide. And this must not happen by chance. There should be no student in any classroom, from kindergarten to graduate school, who feels so isolated that they cannot talk to someone.

What Would You Do?

Kiara is a doctoral student in one of my classes. Although it took me some time, I ultimately learned about her personal struggles. In her 30s, unable to conceive a child of her own, Kiara and her husband adopted a beautiful little girl, Ayana. In fact, one day they received a call from the adoption agency telling them that their baby was about to be born and inviting them to the hospital. Only a few months after Ayana's birth, her adoptive father suffered a series of strokes that left him unable to care for himself. After weeks of struggle, Kiara made the difficult decision to place her husband in a care facility. She leaves her teaching job every day at noon to visit her husband. And daily (except when she has class), she picks up Ayana, now 7, from school, and takes her once again to the care facility to visit her father.

How would the situation of Kiara and Ayana affect their educational experiences?

How might knowing their situations help educators to better relate to, and accommodate, their needs?

Interconnectedness begins at home, with our families, our next-door neighbors, and our co-workers. Yet, we are often oblivious to their lived experiences. We are likely even more oblivious to the fact that we depend on goods and services that come from outside our region or that much of what we rely on for our nourishment, enjoyment, or safety also comes from outside the country. If we simply start by thinking about breakfast, we may enjoy fruit from Florida or California, coffee from Columbia, dairy from Wisconsin, and so on. It might be useful to take a few minutes and begin to reflect on how interconnected our lives are with goods from other countries.

For Reflection

What goods and services do you use on a daily basis and where do they come from?

Food
Clothing
Equipment

Interestingly, our world is so interconnected that some of the goods we export, we also import in large quantities. It may surprise you to know that in 2017, the United States imported $727.7 million worth of rice, but that we also exported rice with a value of $1.8 billion. Similarly, we rarely think about the United States as a huge source of coffee beans, but in 2017, the United States exported $873.1 million in coffee, but was also the world's biggest importer of coffee at US $6.3 billion.

Despite the principal's comment, cited at the beginning of the chapter, that we have everything we need here, this is not actually accurate. In 2017, the United States trade deficit in goods and services was $566 billion. The largest trade deficit was with China, in that many products are made more cheaply there. In fact, although America imports consumer electronics, clothing, and machinery from China, many of these products are actually made by American companies, which ship raw materials to China where they are manufactured at lower cost. When they are transported back to the United States, they are considered imports, even though they still create profit for these US companies.

Interconnectedness, however, is not confined to trade in goods and services, but is related to the worldwide movement of peoples through economic and development initiatives, immigration, asylum seeking, war, and displacement. As previously discussed, most schools have students from many different backgrounds in their classes and it is essential that we develop positive relationships with each of them.

What Would You Do?

In one school in the Detroit area, the majority of students are Yemeni (some first and some second generation), with another large group from Bangladesh, and a smattering of African-American and Caucasian students. In this school, the majority of the female students continue the traditional custom of wearing a full veil during class. Some of the teachers who want to support students support the recommendation of a recent school evaluation team that suggested the school should offer and encourage more vocational training. The rationale was a belief that these students' families do not value education and that most students would not continue formal schooling beyond high school. The assumption was that most of the boys want to get a job to provide a good dowry for their bride and most of the girls will simply be encouraged to get married as they finish high school.

If you were the principal, how would you proceed?
Would you accept the recommendation?
What are your considerations? Who do you talk to?
How do you believe you can best meet the needs of all students?

Interconnectedness with our Past

There is one other form of interdependence that must be taught in schools as we move forward. Russian literary critic Mikhail Bakhtin is concerned that we too often view the past as simply historical, unchanging and unchangeable, and yet, he argues that we must learn to see how it is connected to the present. In other words, although our past and the history of our country has helped to shape us, we must sometimes (often even) learn to re-interpret our assumptions in the light of new knowledge and new understandings. Otherwise, he argues, we will simply accept current interpretations that perpetuate the status quo and that preclude meaningful change.

In other words, we are connected to the historical forces that have shaped our belief systems, our cultures, and our world, but we do not have to accept previous interpretations and injustices. One obvious example is the belief cited from the Texas Ordinance in the previous chapter that the "African race [was] rightfully held and regarded as an inferior and dependent race" (1861). Moreover, this was also the attitude of the US government toward indigenous peoples, who were described by then Chief Justice John Marshall in 1831, as childlike, "domestic dependent nations" and whose relationship to the United States was as a "ward to his guardian."

A similar example that came to the fore again in 2019 was that of the use of minstrelsy and "Blackface." Minstrel shows, first performed in the 1830s (i.e., before the emancipation of slaves), "characterized blacks as lazy, ignorant, superstitious, hypersexual, and prone to thievery and cowardice" (Smithsonian, n.d.). Obviously, these are assumptions that, with a little historical perspective, one realizes must be challenged and certainly not repeated or perpetuated.

For Reflection

What other historical characterizations need to be challenged?

Have you thought about statues, building names, street names, stereotypes?

Did you think about some historical monuments?

What about the confederate flag?

How do we repair insults and injury that we may have previously accepted?

How do some of the current attempts to revise social studies curricula relate to this discussion?

An Example

In Michigan, in 2018, proposed revisions to the social studies curriculum included replacing the phrase "our constitutional democracy" with "our constitutional republic," and removing democratic from the phrase "core democratic values." The instruction "develop and implement an action plan to address or inform others about a public issue" was changed to "inform others about a school issue," thus removing any suggestion of civic participation or responsibility from primary school-age students. In the sixth-grade curriculum, students are asked to investigate a current global issue, although the proposed changes removed suggestions related to climate change, globalization, migration, and human environmental issues. References to the KKK were to be reduced to one; statements related to abortion and gay rights were to be eliminated. As a final example, in the sixth-grade economics section, for the requirement that students consider what products are produced, how, for whom, and for whose benefit, a question that required analysis and critical thinking, was to be eliminated. In other words, there was no longer any suggestion that production might have implications for justice or injustice.

The revisions proposed in Michigan reflected and paralleled changes proposed and sometimes implemented in other states (including Arizona and Texas where changes eliminated references to Martin Luther King and Rosa Parks).

A February 2019 article in the *New York Times* provides a more positive example of the need to revisit history in order to redress omissions and errors. The article described how "African-American women were written out of the history of the woman suffrage movement" (Staples). In fact, many suffragettes and supporters of the women's movement in the nineteenth century, fearing that including African-American women in their petitions or recognizing their efforts would result in the defeat of the bid to gain the vote for women, actually argued that the "disenfranchisement of black women was a race problem—not a gender problem—and beyond the movement's writ." The contributions of many Black women, including Mary Church Terrell and Francis Ellen Watson Harper, are now being "rewritten" into the history of the suffragette movement.

These examples demonstrate the interconnectedness that we must acknowledge and learn about in our public schools. But transformation must go farther. It must acknowledge that interconnectedness is only a beginning. We are truly *interdependent* and must therefore learn to develop trust in one another and to work together despite our differences.

Interdependence

Interdependence occurs on individual human levels throughout our lives (Figure 6.1). We begin by being totally dependent on others for our nourishment, care, and safety. As we develop, we learn how to become independent, while at the same time, acknowledging our interdependence with others. And ultimately, as one ages, the dependence of the child on the adult often reverses as the child becomes a caregiver in turn.

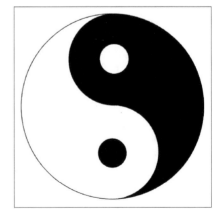

Figure 6.1   Interdependence yin yang.

Interdependence goes beyond interconnectedness and beyond the individual, because it forces us to acknowledge that our very welfare and survival depend on what occurs elsewhere. In May 2011, economist Joseph Stiglitz wrote in *Vanity Fair:*

> [I]n our democracy, 1% of the people take nearly a quarter of the nation's income … In terms of wealth rather than income, the top 1% control 40% … [as a result] the top 1% have the best houses, the best educations, the best doctors, and the best lifestyles, but there is one thing that money doesn't seem to have bought: an understanding that their fate is bound up with how the other 99% live. Throughout history, this is something that the top 1% eventually do learn. Too late.

His closing comment is telling. The fate of the wealthy is bound up with how the other 99% live. The fate of those in the suburbs is bound up with how those in the hearts of our cities live; the fate of those who live in North America is bound up with how those in Nicaragua, Bangladesh, Togo, or China live. And as Stiglitz states, it is to everyone's detriment that we learn that lesson "too late."

In the previous section, we briefly discussed the movement of goods and services between countries, acknowledging that much of what we use every day comes from outside our area. In some cases, without imported goods, we could not have some of the benefits we take for granted in that some resources are not found or produced at all in the United States. One excellent example is bauxite ore, found in Australia, China, and other countries, but not in the United States; bauxite is the major raw material for aluminum production worldwide and is therefore necessary for items we use on a daily basis including cars, refrigerators, electric power lines, computers, and aircraft.

We are also generally well aware of the concept of interdependence in biology in that we know that living things depend on their environments for their needs, including water, nutrition, light, and shelter. Examples include understanding elements of the food chain or studying the relationships between certain animals (deer, giraffes, and cattle) that could not survive without birds that feed on the ticks that hide on their skin.

We know of the importance of preserving wetlands that provide fish and wildlife habitats, improve water quality, or provide a buffer as they store floodwaters. Additionally, we are aware that rainforests that once comprised 20% of the Earth's land surface, today cover less than 7%. Yet, their importance is extreme. Rainforests help to stabilize the world's climate, produce 40% of the earth's oxygen, and are home to over 50% of all known species of living organisms. In many ways, our survival is connected to the well-being of the planet.

When we think about interdependence, I often turn to the award-winning movie *Mardi Gras, Made in China* (available from https://vimeo.com/ondemand/9808). It follows the path of Mardi Gras beads from the factories in Fuzhou, China, where the beads are made, to the streets of New Orleans during Carnival, where revelers are shown partying and exchanging beads for nudity. In the film, we see teenage girls living away from their families and sewing beads together for sixteen hours a day for ten cents an hour, often using outdated and dangerous equipment. The contrast between the carefree and callous comments of revelers and the sacrifices and dangers faced by the workers is an excellent example of globalization at its worst. The North American desire for carefree festivities directly impacts the lives and families of these young workers without most of us ever realizing it.

This is but one example of the ways in which we take the labor of others for granted as we live our daily lives, never realizing the sacrifices others often make for our ease or pleasure.

For Reflection

How does unemployment and illiteracy in my community affect me?

Do I know someone from another country who has come to the United States? Why did they come?

Are there children in my neighborhood school who come from another country? What is their story?

How does immigration along the Texas-Mexico border affect me?

How do the conflicts in Yemen or the Sudan affect me?

How do famine and hardship in Venezuela affect me?

Why does any of this matter?

Each of the foregoing questions could form a prompt for dialogue or a free-writing exercise for faculty, staff, or students, or even an essay assignment for students.

Global Awareness

In the previous chapter, we saw that Robert Dahl identified as one key to a strong democracy the aspect of "enlightened understanding." On a global level, this is sometimes referred to as "global awareness" and even as "global curiosity." Unfortunately, as in the previous example of the school principal, there are some people who seem to have little curiosity or understanding of parts of the globe where they do not live.

Understanding one another is a necessary prerequisite for developing a sense of solidarity and interdependence. It is not enough to simply decide to work together to fulfill a common goal (although

> Solidarity is always motivated by outrage at disparity.
> (Philip Green, 2001)

that may be a useful first step). Research has shown that if a coalition is based simply on strategic considerations it will not last very long; however, if there is a moral commitment and a deep sense of solidarity, the coalition has a better chance of being successful in the longer term. This *egalitarian solidarity*, as Philip Green calls it, is motivated by "outrage at the disparity between the lives of those who possess an immense superfluity and of those many millions more who lack even a bare sufficiency" (2001, p. 176).

For Reflection

What outrages you?
What have you done about it?
What can you do about it?

The foregoing questions may also be asked of a staff of educators within a school, a parent group, or a class of students at any level.

One role of global curiosity is to permit us to better understand situations that may benefit us and those that should outrage us. Global curiosity helps us to identify with people whose reality is different from ours—not from a position of otherness or from a politically correct form of identity politics that maintains separation and difference, but from respect that treats others as equals.

An Example

I once was homeless. I trudged down the streets of a major city with broken down shoes, ripped nylons, and my possessions in a paper shopping bag. Drivers honked their horns. They yelled obscenities at me, offering to hire me for sex. I turned away, trying to ignore the stares and the whistles. I entered a street haven offering a bed and food to homeless women, only to be told that, although I could enjoy their evening meal, there were no beds left. I wandered, resting for a few moments on a park bench or the steps of a church. Each time I thought I was settled for the night, a policeman moved me on, telling me I could not sleep where I was. The police quickly became the enemy as I warily looked for them before settling anywhere. Fortunately, it was May, so I was not cold, although it did start to rain.

The next day, as I shuffled from one bench to another, a "regular" approached me, saying, "You are new here. Do you need help?" He proceeded to tell me the best places for cheap coffee, for free meals at different times of the day, and where I could sometimes, at least, find a bed.

I could never have understood the challenges of being homeless without this experience. I had no concept of the humiliation experienced by women who were being solicited as sex objects. I had never seen the police in this negative light. And I had no sense whatsoever of the camaraderie and helpfulness of those who lived on the street.

For Reflection

Who do you need to get to know better?
How can you begin?
What are your fears?
How can you overcome them?

The point is to ensure we are developing among educators and students both understanding and empathy and not a kind of missionary attitude of superiority. The latter attitude is exemplified in the response of a teacher working on the Navajo reservation in Southeast Utah. When I asked why she had chosen to work in that school, her answer was, "To help the poor little Indians." Quite apart from the offensive use of "Indian," the motivation was appalling. Although quite different from her own, the Navajo culture and lifestyle are rich in traditions and caring relationships, and certainly not to be pitied.

How would you respond to her?

Wanting to engage students to educate them is one thing. Wanting to teach them because you feel sorry for them or pity them is quite another thing. Unless we relate to people with respect and as equals (although with different backgrounds, skills, and cultures) we will fail. Thinking of a group of people as only needing your help, but with nothing to offer in return, essentializes them, relegating them to a persistent position of inferiority and dependency. It is important to become an ally, working *with* others and supporting them as they recognize and extend their talents and capacities and as they also help us to learn and grow.

For Reflection

Why have you chosen your occupation?
Do you have a sense of calling?
What do you hope to accomplish?

Global Curiosity

There is one additional aspect of global curiosity that is important to emphasize. We often stress the disparities in our world between those that have considerable material goods and benefits and those who have little. Yet, once again, we fail to appropriately educate ourselves and our students about the global community if we consign all members of a given group to subordinate categories. For example, in China in 2016, there were still over 43 million people living under the poverty line and earning less than $334 a year in annual income. But the country has been moving rapidly and resolutely to end poverty. In 2002, only 4% of China's population was considered middle class (having enough to satisfy all basic needs with a little left over); in 2016, there were reports that China's population included over 1.34 million millionaires; and by 2022, estimates are that the middle class will increase to 76%. Trade with China is important; their consumer spending is growing at a rate of 14% a year. And this means new markets for developing countries such as the United States as well.

The key point here is that it is as inappropriate to perpetuate images of Chinese women sweeping with homemade straw brooms and wearing "coolie" hats, as it is to present students with images of all Innuit (formerly we called them Eskimos) living in Igloos or all Indigenous Americans living in teepees. Similarly, we must not perpetuate images of all Muslim women wearing "burkas," of all residents of Calcutta living in slums, or of all Fijians wearing grass skirts. I am exaggerating, but the point is that we must not generalize but help students to understand the richness of various communities and cultures beyond our own.

John Law, described in chapter 6 of *Transformative Leadership in Education* (Shields, 2016), not only provided resources for his students to learn about a variety of people in other countries but also to connect with children in more affluent schools like theirs, through electronic means and numerous programs, in order for them to avoid the tendency to essentialize or pity others.

 # Teaching about Interdependence

Educators first need to reflect on why students should think and learn about interdependence and then determine how to teach them. Too often, we support individualistic notions of education and private good, but ignore the interconnectedness of all. A study by Westheimer and Kahn (2004) of different kinds of school programs showed clearly that:

> programs that successfully educate for democracy can promote very different outcomes. Some programs may foster the ability or the commitment to participate, while others may prompt critical analysis that focuses on macro structural issues, the role of interest groups, power dynamics, and/or social justice.
>
> (p. 262)

We must first consider what our goals are and design activities and programs that explicitly and specifically support them. In general, it is important that the activities we propose support and build the capacity of others, that we help students to work *with* and think *with* others, and not *for* them. In other words, once again, we must try to avoid the missionary attitude that suggests others cannot do things for themselves. Thus, a food drive for homeless people might be accompanied by a unit in which students understand the reasons for food scarcity or income disparity in their communities. It might be accompanied by children going to a homeless shelter and interviewing the residents or helping to serve food, so they become acquainted with real people instead of simply tossing a few dollars (often given to them by their parents) into a jar.

For Reflection

How can you introduce more activities that promote global awareness and an understanding of interdependence into your units in age- and grade-appropriate ways?

 ## What Can Transformative Educators Do?

1. To promote an understanding of interconnectedness and interdependence, educators are well aware of various games and activities that

build trust. These include activities in which students are paired, one is blindfolded, and both are asked to complete a task; games in which pairs sit back to back and one describes a shape while the other draws it sight unseen; or scavenger hunts and other kinds of activities that can relate to any desired topic.

2. Many educators have also used a variation of what is known as a jigsaw activity in which students first meet in small groups with participants numbered from 1–4 (assuming four people in each group) (Figure 6.2). Following some time spent together, all those numbered 1 get together, the 2s meet together, and so on, to delve deeper into an

Figure 6.2 Jigsaw.

aspect of the task. Ultimately, everyone returns to the original group to share insight. (Those who might be unfamiliar with this activity will find details in the eResources.) The jigsaw game activity actually began in 1971 in an attempt to defuse the racial tensions present at a school in Austin, Texas, which had recently integrated. It points once again to the importance of getting to know those who are different from ourselves and sharing a task with them, in order to promote understanding and respect.

3. To support educators in helping students understand important global facts, there are many excellent free resources available. One of my favorites is an excellent newsletter called "Get Connected," produced by the Australian branch of the international charity, *World Vision*. This award-winning newsletter produces various issues that cover topics such as global citizenship, climate change, water in the world, and so on. It contains excellent information and activities for children in grades five through ten and will be generally useful for schools whether they are in Australia or not. The newsletter is available free, and anyone can subscribe by going to their website *⊘*.

The activities include information summaries where students are asked to fill in the blanks, puzzles, games, dramas, stories, role-play activities, service activities, reflective activities, and so on. Check out the issue called "Global Citizenship" *⊘*. This issue emphasizes the United Nations development goals, multiple activities, and aspects of citizenship, and promotes both creative and critical thinking. The description of the Peace Camp in Lebanon highlights once again how working with those who at first seem "different" permits us to move from mistrust of one another to confident and productive relationships.

4. The issue about global citizenship provides maps and charts of world demographics and in multiple ways invites students to consider their place in the world. One set of activities asks students to imagine that they live in a village of 100 people, a village that represents the global community. In that village, we are shown the breakdown of the population by nationality and by religion. And we are told that of the 100 people,

- 43 live without basic sanitation
- 7 are educated at a secondary level
- 14 cannot read
- 52 live on $2 a day or less
- 18 have an internet connection
- 18 live without an improved water source
- 18 are hungry or malnourished.

Students could be asked to write about, discuss, or even role play what life would be like in that village, which amenity they might not have, and what their friends' lives might be like.

5. Using the "Get Connected" resources related to climate change, students may be asked to understand the differences between climate and weather, to trace the incidents of natural disasters in various parts of the world, and to try to explain them. Why, for example, was much of the United States covered by a polar vortex in the winter of 2019? Why have natural disasters increased in this century? Why do people argue that we need to decrease the use of fossil fuels? Students might even engage in informed debate about whether humans influence climate change.

6. You might encourage students to explore some of the disparities in the global village. If they ask why so many people are hungry or illiterate, or living without basic sanitation, it would also be important to ensure students do not generalize these issues to whole populations but that they understand in every country, just as in theirs, there are poor, middle-class, and wealthy people. You could ask students to watch the video, "What Causes Poverty?" 🔗

7. In a science unit, one might ask students to monitor and estimate the amount of water they use in a day, to learn about water management strategies at home and abroad, and to explore the impact of not having

clean or potable water on a family or community. Once again, one can teach the prescribed curriculum and, at the same time, ensure that students develop broader, socially-just just understandings about the world in which they live.

Assessing Progress

To assess progress in promoting awareness and understanding of interconnectedness, interdependence, and global curiosity, one can use a variety of measures. To assess educators' awareness and comfort with these ideas, one might watch whether teachers begin to sit with and interact with others outside their regular group. You might also ask for sharing of strategies or lesson plans at a staff meeting.

For students, assessing progress might include:

- Evaluating students' answers about global issues on teacher-made tests.
- Having students complete activities such as those found in *Get Connected.*
- Assessing the ability of students to complete crossword puzzles and other activities related to concepts discussed.
- Monitoring student interactions with classmates who come from different ethnic, linguistic, cultural, or religious groups: who sits together in the cafeteria? Who is chosen as a partner, and so on?
- Monitoring disciplinary incidents between students from different groups.

Concluding Thoughts

Philip Green (2001) states that

> Life is fuller for all of us when we live it among *different* people, all respecting and identifying with each other in that difference. … That life, of cooperation with others of different experiences in seeking common goals, is also the only kind of life that will create the institutions of equal opportunity.
>
> (pp. 185–186)

He insists that it is important to develop empathy for others, not because they share our ethnic, linguistic, or cultural identity, or our talents and abilities, but because "that person is an individual and no individual should be unjustly deprived of rights" (p. 188).

I came to empathize more with those who are homeless, not because I can truly understand their situation, but because I shared it briefly.

An Example Continued

Now, in the name of full disclosure, I need to tell you that my "homelessness" was temporary—part of a three-day plunge in which I (and other participants) had been given $3.00 and told to remain within a certain geographic "high poverty" area in a large city for a long weekend. Yet, I have never forgotten the rude looks, the leering catcalls, the rough treatment by the police, and the general rejection I experienced during those three days.

For Reflection

What experiences have you had that have helped you to better empathize with others?

How can you share what you learned with others?

How have you, or can you, put it into practice?

This chapter has emphasized the collective and interdependent nature of the world, and the need for our education system to ensure that learning is not simply a solitary activity consisting of passing tests and memorizing information. Because education is the foundation of a healthy, prosperous, and sustainable civil, democratic, and global society, transformative educators must work to end educational benefits that accrue only to certain privileged individuals who acquire knowledge, skills, and attitudes to enable their success. The exploration of each foundational yet broad global value that comprises Tenet Six has extended the discussion, begun in the previous chapter, of how schools may be reconstructed in transformative ways, addressing policies as well as curricula to ensure the inclusion of multiple perspectives.

 # References

Green, P. (2001), Egalitarian solidarity, In S. J. Goodlad (Ed.), *The last best hope*. San Francisco, CA: Jossey-Bass, pp. 176–193.

Hames-Garcia, M. R. (2000), Who are our own people? Challenges for a theory of social identity. In P. M. L. Moya, & M. R. Hames-Garcia (Eds.), *Reclaiming identity: Realist theory and the predicament of postmodernism*. Berkeley, CA: University of California Press, pp. 102–129.

Shields, C. M. (2016), *Transformative leadership in education*, 2nd ed., New York: Routledge.

Smithsonian. (n.d.), American blackface: The birth of an American stereotype, National Museum of African American History and Culture. accessed February 2019 at https://nmaahc.si.edu/blog-post/blackface-birth-american-stereotype.

Staples, B. (2019), When the suffrage movement sold out to White supremacy, *New York Times*, February 2, 2019. accessed February 2019 at www.nytimes.com/2019/02/02/opinion/sunday/women-voting-19th-amendment-white-supremacy.html.

Stiglitz, J. E. (2011), Of the 1%, by the 1%, for the 1%, *Vanity Fair*. accessed March 2015 at www.vanityfair.com/news/2011/05/top-one-percent-201105.

Texas Ordinance of Secession. (1861), Lone Star Junction. accessed April 2019 at www.lsjunction.com/docs/secesson.htm.

Westheimer, J., & Kahn, J. (2004), What kind of citizen? The politics of educating for democracy, *American Educational Research Journal*, 41(2), 237–269.

Tenet Seven
Balancing Critique and Promise

*This seventh tenet of transformative leadership theory emphasizes some important dispositions and actions that must be considered in order to create schools that are inclusive, equitable, excellent, and socially just. It posits the importance of a **critical** theory of leadership that includes both critique and promise in order to implement and sustain transformation.*

This seventh tenet undergirds the rest. Whether we are seeking to redress power imbalances or to ensure an adequate emphasis on democracy or interconnectedness, we must do so using the dual approaches of critiquing the status quo and of offering the promise and the possibility of something better.

> Leadership that is "critically educative" not only looks at the conditions in which we live, but it must also decide how to change them.
> (William Foster, 1986)

Hence, the majority of this chapter will comprise vignettes that may be analyzed and discussed in terms of identifying and critiquing the challenges and problems facing transformative leaders and thinking about promising ways forward. First, however, the chapter provides a brief discussion of the meaning of these key terms and of the importance of a *critical* theory of leadership.

Critical Theories of Leadership

When we think about *critical* or *radical* theories of leadership, it is important to note that all share a focus on *justice* and on foregrounding those individuals or groups who have historically and persistently suffered inequities, marginalization, or oppression. The distinguishing feature of any critical theory is that it focuses on the lived experiences of the least advantaged and least successful in society and attempts to both explain and to rectify their inequitable situations. Additionally, and importantly, critical theory addresses ideological forces and structures that (re)produce and perpetuate inequity.

In reality, there are multiple critical theories—but all begin by seeking the emancipation and liberation of the least powerful, the most marginalized in our society. These critical theories include critical race theories (Collins, 1991; Lynn & Parker, 2006), critical queer theories (Capper, 1998: Sears, 1993), critical feminist theories (Elsworth, 1989; Kenway & Modra, 1992), and so on. Sometimes, the term radical instead of critical is used as in radical post-structuralism or radical servant leadership (Letizia, 2014).

Transformative leadership is a critical leadership theory. Sometimes one sees, in the literature, the phrase, "critical transformative leadership," although this is technically not necessary because the theory is inherently *critical* in that the starting point is to identify those groups that have been marginalized in our society and rectify beliefs and practices that perpetuate the marginalization. Thus, transformative leadership differs from many other leadership theories, including many iterations of leadership for social justice or culturally relevant or responsive leadership, in that it goes beyond trying to ensure a socially just education for all students, to critique, deconstruct, and work to transform structural and societal inequities and disparities. It requires that those with privilege (adults, youth, and children) acknowledge their role in the perpetuation of social injustice and begin to accept their responsibility to become allies and agents of transformation.

For Reflection

What groups or individuals can you identify that have been marginalized?

In your school?
In your community?
Your global village?

Develop a comprehensive list of inequities with students and ask them to create and display posters for the classroom wall.

Thinking about Critique

The concept of *critique* is closely related to the concept of critical theory in that *critique* is neither a synonym for negative and unproductive criticism, nor is it synonymous with "critical thinking." Critique comes from a Greek word meaning "skilled in judging" and implies a thoughtful examination of the merits of something. It therefore requires the transformative leader to develop and exercise skill in judging what is working and what is not working, in identifying who is privileged and who is marginalized, in order to fulfil the deeply democratic purposes of public schooling.

A *critique* is an evaluation of something so it can be better understood by others. It implies that one understands a topic, evaluates its various components (positive and negative), and presents it in an understandable format. Hence, if you want to critique the omnipresence of standardized tests, you would need to know something of their history and intended purpose, what they actually can demonstrate, how they are often misused, and how they may be biased toward particular groups of test-takers. You cannot simply show what is wrong with standardized testing but would have to offer ideas for improvement and redress as well.

The aim of transformative leadership theory is broad: to increase school success, emancipation, democracy, equity, and justice for all groups of students who experience marginalization, including those who are racialized, poor, LGBTQ, from a non-dominant religious or language group, experience physical or mental challenges, and so forth. Transformative leadership is a way of embracing all students, encouraging them to know and to be proud of their identities. In New Zealand, one of the mantras of those who work with Māori students is that they must learn to *succeed as Māori*. Success without sacrificing one's identity is essential. And this kind of success requires teaching students about the social construction and perpetuation of inequity and how this may be changed.

Transformative leaders critique and redress positions and perspectives, structures and cultures, policies and practices, that result in any form of oppression or inequity. Although the starting point for positive transformation may well be critique, it will also require effort, strategies, and courage to create more socially just and inclusive organizations.

Thinking about Promise

Although some writers use the term "possibilities," I use the term *promise* because it is an adjective, a noun, and a verb. As an adjective, we often hear of people receiving a promise ring as a symbol of a relationship; a promise card, reminding the recipient of the sender's intent to do something; or even the "promised land"—suggesting a place of wealth and happiness. As a noun, a promise is an assurance that something will (or will not) be done. It implies a solemn pledge made by someone who is trustworthy and whom you can trust, as in "I will keep my promise to always treat you with respect." And as a verb, promise is the assurance of action to be taken to accomplish an agreed-upon purpose, as in "I promise to be at your birthday party."

Related to transformative leadership, therefore, once one critiques a policy, an action, a structure, an attitude, and so on, careful reflection and solicitous action are required. *Promise* implies hope, possibility, and future action. It implies a contract in which transformative leaders undertake to serve their constituency—*all* members of their school community, as expressed in the words of the US Constitution, "we the people ...." It does not state, "we the White people" or "we the rich people, but simply "the people."

To ensure the promise of transformative leadership, educators may be encouraged to engage in such activities as examining various policies and practices, holding open fora or town hall meetings with various

Figure 7.1 Hands of promise.

groups, advocating for specific partnerships with community groups, and, in general, speaking out with ideas for moving forward to create better, more excellent, and more equitable schools. I call the image in Figure 7.1 "Hands of promise" in that it shows brightly colored hands, each with a word representing a human right or promise (freedom, peace, hope, dignity, promise, justice, democracy, rights, equity). Let us join our hands with theirs.

As indicated previously, one way to think about promise is to institute the use of "promise cards" by faculty, staff, students, and community members. These cards may be used in many different ways. One may write down a promise to someone and simply give or send them the card. Another way to build trusting relationships is to have two people exchange promise cards with one another, emphasizing an agreement between them. In some cases, it is useful to write a message to oneself and have someone you trust mail it on a given date as a reminder of a promise you need to keep.

Write a promise card to someone and share it appropriately.

Building Organizational Trust

There is little doubt that trust is closely related to promise-giving and promise-keeping and is a necessary foundation upon which to build relationships and to enter into partnerships that may result in change. One important aspect of engaging in a combination of both critique and promise is that they both rely on trust and help to build it.

Between 1999 and 2001, scholars Hoy and Tschannen-Moran studied the research on organizational trust and ultimately defined it as:

> a state in which groups are willing to make themselves vulnerable to others and take risks with full confidence that others will respond in positive ways, that is, with benevolence, reliability, competence, honesty, and openness.
>
> (Hoy, 2012, p. 81)

As a starting point, it is clear that trust depends on others believing in the promise that you will act with benevolence (kindness), reliability, honesty, and openness. Moreover, as the need for competence suggests, there are times when good intentions are not sufficient, and when skill and knowledge are particularly important. All of these characteristics are fundamental to being able to engage in both honest critique and promise regarding a particular situation. Moreover, this kind of trust implies that one trusts someone else **to do** something. Here an example might be to assume that once a school leader says he or she will look into a situation or take a particular action or refrain from a particular course of action, one can rely on his or her word.

A few years later, Hoy and Tschannen-Moran refined their definition of trust and added an additional component: collective trust **in** students and parents (p. 82). They found, as had other researchers, that collective trust in students and parents was positively associated with increased student achievement (even though collective trust in colleagues was not statistically significant).

What does trust in parents mean?
How does it relate to the elimination of deficit thinking?
Why is this kind of trust essential?

Trust in students and parents implies more than just assuming they will keep their word. It implies a rejection of deficit thinking and a strong belief that everyone is working to the best of his or her ability to fulfill the familial, societal, and educational roles assigned to them. In other words, we must believe that teachers are doing the best they know how to do, that par-

> Education is the most powerful weapon which you can use to change the world.
>
> (Nelson Mandela)

ents are working hard to love and support their children to their utmost ability, and that students really do want to learn and are trying, as well as they know how, to cooperate and fulfill the expectations of the school.

This kind of trust may stretch the credulity of some educators, but it is the foundation on which critique and promise can truly work. Our starting point must be to believe that we are all partners in the important endeavor of education—the endeavor that Nelson Mandela termed the most powerful weapon we have to change the world. And to begin the transformation, we need to think about how we might engage in both critique and promise in common situations.

What Would You Do?

The following vignettes are intended for discussion and reflection. The first two include a relatively detailed analysis, while the last two provide less analysis to leave room for more investigation and dialogue by groups of educators.

Vignette 1. A School Principal's Dilemma

Principal Herman had been the formal leader of Hopeful High School for over twenty years. In the past ten years, he noticed that the population of 1300 students had changed significantly—from 80% White to over 50% African American, 30% Latinx, and 10% other non-White immigrant and newcomer groups. However, 95% of the teachers were White; one dean was Black and one assistant principal was Latina. 60% of the students qualified for free and reduced-price lunch;

30% of the students spoke a language other than English at home. About twenty-five girls in the school wore hijabs and three others came fully veiled. In short, the school resembled many twenty-first century high schools throughout America.

Although there were no overt signs of conflict among the students, there were indications of emerging tensions. The school's reputation was changing from an "academic school" in which most students were "college-bound" to a "minority-majority school" with a reputation for athletic achievement. Test scores were falling. An unprecedented number of teachers in the previous five years had asked for transfers. Parents and students alike complained that the meals in the cafeteria were not appropriate for all students and urged the board to offer vegetarian meals as well as to eliminate pork and pork products from the menu. Members of the community became aware of an increasing rate of suspensions, especially for African-American students who were often described by teachers as "louder, more sociable, and more high spirited" than their peers. A few teachers wanted principal Herman to institute a policy that required everyone show their face, claiming they could not teach girls who were veiled. However, Principal Herman did not want to create a policy that might be seen to blame the changing demographics and single out certain groups and so he talked in general terms about the need to pay attention to everyone, and about the need for diversity training. In fact, he ensured that several of the school's teachers participated in the district's diversity committee. He successfully encouraged several non-White parents to participate in the parent council, although it was still dominated by relatively affluent White professional parents and business owners. And he took pride in both the multicultural fair and the Black student-run assembly presented for the previous three years during Black History Month. So, he was confused when a local paper ran a story indicating that at the root of the school's problems was racial tension and that he and the school had not done enough to create an equitable, inclusive, and excellent environment for all students. At that point, principal Herman decided that it was time he retired.

You are the new principal of the high school.
How do you offer critique and promise?
What could you do differently?

Some Points of Analysis

Recall that offering a critique has been defined as being skilled in judgment in order to offer a thoughtful examination of the merits of something. It implies analyzing something so it can be better understood by others.

How would you, as the newly appointed principal, summarize your thinking to the staff, the district, and the community? If you were to conduct a SWOT analysis of the school, what might appear on each list? What data would you need to use to be clear and convincing?

Of course, there are no right or wrong answers, and some items I consider to be threats, you might see as opportunities and so on; however, hopefully, you would consider most, if not all of, the points listed in Table 7.1.

It appears obvious that there is much to build on here, but there are also some threats and increasing weaknesses that must be taken seriously. Thinking about the previously discussed first six tenets of transformative leadership might give the new principal some guidance in terms of where and how to start. What might the answers be if (s)he was to ask the staff to examine the SWOT chart and to answer the questions posed in the introduction?

It might become apparent that although there were a few school-wide events that highlighted the African-American population, these were one-off activities and not fully embedded in the life of the school. There did not seem to be any particular recognition of the Muslim or newcomer community. Moreover, the changing student population had brought some negative responses from the teachers (African Americans are loud, we cannot teach girls who are veiled, we need to transfer). Yet, despite these comments, Mr. Herman, in a misplaced desire to "keep the peace," was reluctant to talk about race or racism and so couched the need for change in a discussion of diversity (as yet undefined). Here the need for adopting tenet 2—the

Table 7.1　A SWOT Analysis for Vignette 1

Strengths	Weaknesses	Opportunities	Threats
No overt conflict	Little diversity of staff	Cafeteria meals	Teacher transfers
Strong athletic program	Test scores declining	Teacher perceptions of African Americans and Muslims	Increased community awareness of suspensions
Former excellent reputation	Increased African-American suspensions	Newspaper interested in the school	
Diverse student population		Principal talked about diversity but could be specific about race and racism	Failure to name racism
Diverse parent council		Linguistic diversity	Council dominated by White parents
Teachers on district diversity committee			
Multicultural fair			
Black student-led assembly			

need to deconstruct mindsets and knowledge frameworks that perpetuate diversity and to reconstruct them in more equitable ways—is at the forefront. Similarly, although Mr. Herman had been able to encourage some non-White parents to join the parent council, it was still dominated by well-educated, articulate, and powerful White parents; hence the need for tenet 3: the redistribution of power in more equitable ways.

What questions might be asked of the teachers to help them understand why they believed they could not teach girls wearing veils or why the school's reputation was declining? What strategies could you use to support the teachers? How might you convince parents that you understood and were supportive of their concerns? How might you engage the author of the newspaper article to help promote a deeper understanding of the changed and changing school community and to bring people together?

Key Equity Questions

Who is excluded and who is included?
Who is advantaged and who disadvantaged?
Who is marginalized and who privileged?
Whose voices have been heard and whose have been silenced?

Here, to bring the promise of a school that is inclusive, excellent, equitable, and socially just into effect, it will be necessary to help teachers understand why they perceive African-American and Muslim students differently from others. It will be essential to engage in dialogue that names racism and discrimination if the disproportionate rate of suspensions is to be addressed. An analysis of the pedagogical program (tenets 5 and 6) will be important to determine whether everyone in the school has access to a high level of instruction and advanced, college preparatory programs or whether perceived language barriers have resulted in the over-placement of English language learner students in lower-level classes (tenets 1, 5, and 6). How can non-White parents be assured more voice and more responsibility at the parent council and would co-chairs help the situation? And are discrete events related to multiculturalism adequate, or given the school's new demographic make-up, how can every aspect of the school reflect the diversity of its families and students?

The answers to these and other questions will have to be found by those who share responsibility for the school programs—educators, students, parents, and the community as a whole. But I am reminded of the responses of two schools—one elementary and one high school—to some of these questions. (See eResources for pictures of these schools.) One elementary school in Denver, Colorado, that wanted to better communicate its values to the wider community, filled the school from foyer to classrooms with visuals, and even painted the school crest and mascot on the street leading to the school and on the exterior walls of the school for all who passed to see.

The high school, located in Monument Valley, Utah, comprised a student population that was almost 100% Navajo. On one occasion, educators from the State Office of Education, having spent a day visiting the school, commented as they left that it was a "wonderful school that looked just like any other school in the state." Although meant as a compliment, the savvy principal immediately recognized the problem. It was not just like any other school, and so she set out to make changes—Navajo paintings on the walls and pillars, a churro sheep and traditional weaving project, an ethno-botany garden, the construction of a shade house and a hooghan for meetings and important events—all depicted on the web to help you imagine what you might do in your school.

For Reflection

When you walk into your school, what do you see?
Who is represented? What values are obvious?
How does your school reflect pride in its student body?
What makes it equitable, inclusive, excellent, and socially just?
What might you need to change?

▪ Vignette 2. A Disputed Policy

An increased pressure for accountability and college readiness on the part of the state had caused considerable concern among the general population that too many students were not exhibiting grade-level competence on the state-mandated standardized tests. Legislators had been convinced of the truth of the aphorism that "until 3rd grade, students learn to read, but that after third grade, they read to learn." Hence, after considerable debate in the assembly, it was decided to introduce a mandatory policy of retaining students who were not reading at grade level at the end of third grade. However, in recognition that there was an increasingly large number of students entering the state's schools who came from other countries, some of whom did not speak English and a few who had never had the prior opportunity to attend school, the policy indicated that these students could have one additional year of schooling before being retained.

As expected, there was mixed support for the policy, with many teachers and parents expressing support and others concerned that the outcome would be a differential impact on students based on race and social status. In fact, after one year of implementation, it was found that urban, African-American, and Latinx students were being retained four times as often as White students or students who lived outside the state's major urban centers.

> You are a third-grade teacher. How do you offer both critique and promise?

Points of Analysis

Whereas in the case of Hopeful High School, the starting point for the principal may have been to address underlying beliefs and mindsets, here the strategy will need to be different. You, as a third-grade teacher, may be concerned about the legislation, but one voice will likely have little impact, although one person can certainly start the ball rolling. Hence, there is a need for collective action and for determining who has the power and influence to make a difference.

The first step to addressing any concerns related to this legislation is to understand the legislation and to *gather research and data* related to its impact. For example, it may be important to know that sixteen states have some form of required retention and/or intervention for failure to read at grade level by the end of the third grade, and eight additional states permit retention but do not require it. Nationally, in 2016, 82% of African-American fourth graders were reading below proficiency, along with 79 and 78% of Latino and American Indian students respectively, and 79% of those who qualified for free and reduced-price lunch (NCSL, 2018). The legislated retention solution is, of course, controversial, with some strongly in support and others concerned that third-grade retention is associated with subsequent high rates of dropping out and/or lack of high school completion.

In Michigan, for example, prior to similar legislation being passed, it was noted that "less than half of Michigan third graders attained a passing score, called proficient, on the reading portion" of the mandated standardized test. The proposed solution was to retain all students who were one or more grade levels behind in reading at the end of the third grade. Public Act 306 of 2016 was intended to go into full force in the 2019–2020 school year and contained a number of qualifications and possible exclusions under the "good cause exemption" clauses. It was also an "unfunded mandate" in that it required that every district have an "identified early literacy coach" and mandated that every student receive more minutes of reading instruction than they had the previous year, but without providing an additional funding to schools.

A cursory examination of the tenets in play here indicates the relevance of most tenets including the need: 1) for a mandate for change; 2) to deconstruct knowledge about retention; 3) to redistribute power; 4) to balance public and private good; and 5) to ensure that the education received by all students emphasized emancipation, democracy, and equity.

The equity challenges of the legislation include exorbitant additional costs for districts (estimated to be at $10,700 per retained student) as well as the fact that there is an over-representation of minoritized students (African American, Latinx, impoverished) being retained. Moreover, one result of blaming teachers and schools is the proliferation of for-profit charter schools and high-cost tutoring services that may be accessed by more affluent parents to ensure their child will not be retained. Yet, the preponderance of evidence from decades of research and hundreds of studies "argues that students who repeat a grade are no better off, and are sometimes worse off, than if they had been promoted with their classmates" (David, 2008).

There is no doubt, based on the statistics, that there is a reading problem; however, it would be useful to learn to ask the following questions when examining any policy or proposed solution for an agreed-upon problem.

For Reflection

For what problem is that (in this case retention) a solution?
What are other ways to address the problem?
Who has the power to persuade?
Do we need to mobilize the community?
If so, how can we mobilize the community?

If transformative educators are to offer promise in this situation, knowing that, in general, repeating the same situation does not bring different results, there must be other options. This is especially true given the research finding that in general students still struggle during the repeated year, are faced with the additional stigma of having been retained, and two years later, show no advantage over those who have not been retained (David, 2008).

A third-grade teacher armed with data and some possible alternative solutions might first enlist the support of some teaching peers, discuss with the principal the wisdom of holding a public town hall meeting at which some local legislators might be invited, and develop a short monograph of information related to the situation. Inviting prominent local business owners (who obviously have an interest in well-educated employees) and knowledgeable researchers might also provide useful perspectives. The point is that reversing legislation that is inequitable and has a demonstrably disproportionate negative impact on several groups in the community requires wide public support and activism.

What are some promising alternative solutions?

Here you might propose

- A reading clinic offered by a local university for additional teacher training
- Moving to a balanced calendar with intensive literacy instruction for those below grade level during inter-session classes

- Summer school or reading camps for students who need additional support
- Home-based intervention even prior to kindergarten
- Programs to teach parents how to help with reading at home
- A modification of the reading curriculum to include small group dialogue and inquiry.

To mobilize the community, one might learn from a small school in Florida which, some years ago, instituted various programs to enlist the support of parents. On a regular day each week, they had activities such as Monday muffins in which parents came, shared coffee and muffins, and were given a tip about how to help their child. On a different day, perhaps Wednesday, they had a different activity to involve parents in their children's education.

To modify the reading program, one might explore Pogrow's (2009) research on school failure that posits that the "chief culprit is reliance on remedial basic skill/test prep instruction" and offers instead a practice of teaching both reading and thinking skills through small-group conversation and dialogue.

There are always alternatives and it is important for transformative leaders to reflect on solutions that offer promise and not punishment to those who need assistance.

Vignette 3. A "Failing Student"

Jarrod is a student in a fifth-grade class. He comes to school wearing the same t-shirt all week, hair unbrushed, and often, despite the cold and snowy winter, wearing only a light windbreaker and worn out sneakers. You have recently learned that he lives, with his father and younger brother, in a single room with a two-burner hotplate and a bathroom at the end of the hall. During his mother's struggle with cancer (and before her death), his father had lost his job and subsequently their house, trying to provide the necessary medicine and support to his wife. Jarrod seems bright enough but he is reading at only a third-grade level and his math skills test at the second-grade level. At the same time, you are aware that

Jarrod helps his father shop and cook dinner, and that he has been able to help almost every other resident of the building to fix a broken doorknob, or a rusty light switch, and sometimes even has managed to help them connect to the building's ancient and unreliable internet. The school counselor has just come to you to suggest that because is failing, Jarrod should be transferred out of your class and into a remedial program in another building that focuses on life skills.

If you are the teacher, how do you offer critique and promise in this situation?
What do you do if you are the principal?

Which tenets are engaged here? Here, once again, the mandate for change seems to be accompanied by a need to deconstruct knowledge frameworks, for examining the use of power, the need for both public and private good, and again, for an education that is democratic and equitable. Here, however, I will make only a few comments and leave the deeper analysis to the reader.

In this vignette, there are a lot of assumptions suggested by Jarrod's situation that one finds in many schools across the country—assumptions about students who are homeless, about *opportunity to learn* as opposed to *ability to learn*, and about the utility of remedial programs. We also know that Jarrod has insight and technical skills; he seems bright and has not demonstrated any particular discipline problems. Once again, the question—*for what problem is that a solution*—becomes important. What benefit would there be for Jarrod to be moved away from his teacher, friends, and classmates, given the disruption he has already experienced, and placed in a remedial program? In what ways would the remedial program help him to catch up and then to develop his potential. Recall Gabriel's story in Chapter 2 and ask what kind of support and assistance would truly help Jarrod to thrive. Reflect on the response of the teacher in *Transformative Leadership in Education* (Shields, 2016) who informed a homeless child that orange juice was not a food and hence that he could not use it to fulfill the requirements of a social study project.

A school principal once noticed a child who came to school a bit disheveled like Jarrod, wearing a t-shirt with a stain on it, day after day. She called the mother and asked what the school could do to help, wondering if she had detergent and access to a washing machine, and offering support. At that, the mother burst into tears during the phone call. Worried, the principal asked if everything was all right and if she had said something to upset the mother. The parent's response was to say that this was the first time she had ever received a call from a school offering help, instead of criticism. This principal had clearly offered the promise that every educator can offer through a well-placed word or simply a phone call.

Vignette 4. Increasing Parent Involvement

> You are the community-liaison person for a small charter-school district with one elementary, one middle, and one high school. The district primarily draws parents from immigrant families recently arrived from war-torn and conflicted areas of the globe, primarily Yemen, Bangladesh, and Syria. The manager of the charter-school company is a former director of an insurance company who has recently been hired by the corporation to improve achievement as well as to ensure that the schools return a profit for the shareholders. He has instructed you to improve parental involvement in the schools because he has read that "when parents are involved, students achieve more …." You have tried to convince more parents to attend parent-teacher meetings by sending notices in multiple community languages and by offering both translators and child-care for children under five, but to this point, you have been largely unsuccessful in changing the "dismal" rate of parental involvement.

> How do you offer critique and promise in this situation?

Once again, when one reflects on this situation, it is apparent that it invokes the principles of several tenets of transformative leadership theory, including the mandate for change, the need for new knowledge frameworks, the use of power, the creation of a democratic education for all, and, in this case, the importance of global awareness and understanding.

For Reflection

Here, it behooves educators to reflect carefully on the following questions:

Is there a problem?
What is the problem?
How is the problem being defined?
What outcomes are desired?
Who will benefit and who might be disadvantaged?

Hopefully this analysis will result in educators understanding that "involvement" can take many forms and that for many immigrant families, involvement is confined to what they do at home, respectfully leaving educational matters to the "experts." In other words, telling children to be on time, supervising homework, supporting the need for education—even to the point of telling them they do not want to spend their lives on the menial tasks often completed by newcomers—are all ways parents indicate they support education. As we saw when we examined Aline's situation in the discussion of Tenet Three having translators and sending newsletters home in languages of the community may be excellent first steps, but more is needed.

If we truly consider tenet 6 that asks us to develop understanding of interconnectedness, inter-relationships, and global awareness, we will want to learn more about the family, their background, their culture, and their prior experiences with schooling and education. We will listen to their challenges, hopes, and aspirations. Nevertheless, too often, schools wanting to increase parental involvement do so on their terms, or on White middle-class terms, and offer only one-way communication that *tells* parents what the school wants them to know or to do, but fails to *ask* parents what they want from the school or how the school can support them or their child.

Transforming the ways in which we think about and conceptualize parental involvement, developing truly trusting relationships and partnerships, can result in considerable widespread support for, and involvement in, the life of the school.

Assessing Progress

Although one cannot *measure* progress toward ensuring a combination of both critique and promise in our schools, it is possible to find indicators of progress. If no-one raises the questions proposed earlier regarding who benefits, who is advantaged, and who might be disadvantaged by a particular decision, then obviously more work needs to be done. On the other hand, if you note some of the following, then you are making progress:

- You can record an increase in the participation of various groups in decision making.
- More perspectives are being considered when addressing challenges.
- You can walk into your school and see some visual representations of the students who comprise the student body and what the school values.
- Someone proposes a quick solution to a situation and the questions of "For what problem is that a solution?" or "What other options do we have" are asked.
- When a problem is found, someone asks, "What data are available and what do we still need to know?"
- Once you have agreed upon a course of action, it is implemented without delay.

Moving Forward

This chapter demonstrates that the tenets of transformative leadership theory come into play in most, if not all, of the challenging situations faced by educators on a day-to-day basis. I could have added vignettes about resource allocation, personnel decisions, facility needs, and so on. In every case, one would have to ask the questions of advantage and disadvantage, of inclusion and marginalization.

Similarly, in almost every case, there will be a need to accept a mandate for deep and equitable change, to challenge existing assumptions, mindsets, and knowledge frame-

> The language of critique should always contain the language of possibility and the language of possibility should always contain the language of critique.
>
> (Quantz, Rogers, & Dantley, 1991)

works, to redistribute power, and to ensure that the education being offered to all children is democratic and equitable, taking into account global perspectives and interconnectedness. There will be a need to ensure that public and private good are balanced, that both critique and promise are deep-rooted. Thus, it should have become apparent that the tenets of transformative leadership theory help to provide a focus for critique as well as offer ways to inform positive action that offers redress.

It has also become clear that in almost every case, there will be some pushback and disagreement. When making decisions focused on the redistribution of resources in more equitable ways, there will almost always be opposition by those who are already advantaged by the status quo.

Quantz, Rogers, and Dantley (1991) reminded us of the importance of ensuring that educators *believe* that change can occur. But they also argue that "it is not enough to provide a vision of the future" because one must also "recognize how to work within the present to move toward that vision" (p. 108). Moreover, they posit that "for transformational [sic] leadership to actually transform, it must cause individuals to question the assumptions upon which the 'vision' is based" (p. 97). This is where critique comes in. Once again, as stated at the beginning of this chapter, critique involves a careful analysis of both present and historical forces and mechanisms that work against the goals of equity, inclusion, excellence, and social justice. Critique does not allocate blame, but offers a comprehensive understanding of the reality of a situation. Hence, the goal of this chapter was to demonstrate how reflection and dialogue may be used as strategies to ensure that critique and promise are always intertwined in ways that offer hope for a better future. Moreover, to accomplish the kind of transformation discussed in these chapters requires a considerable dose of moral courage.

 # References

Capper, C. A. (1998), Critically oriented and postmodern perspectives: Sorting out the differences and applications for practice, *Educational Administration Quarterly, 34*(3), 354–379.

Collins, P. H. (1991), *Black feminist thought: Knowledge, consciousness, and the politics of empowerment.* New York: Routledge.

David, J. L. (2008), What Research Says About ... / Grade Retention, *Educational Leadership, 65*(6), 83–84. accessed February 2019 at www. ascd.org/publications/educational-leadership/mar08/vol65/num06/Gra de-Retention.aspx.

Ellsworth, E. (1989), Why doesn't this feel empowering? Working through the repressive myths of critical pedagogy, *Harvard Educational Review, 59*(3), 297–323.

Foster, W. (1986), *Paradigms and promises.* Buffalo, NY: Prometheus.

Hoy, W. (2012), School characteristics that make a difference for the achievement of all students: A 40-year odyssey, *Journal of Educational Administration, 50*(1), 76–97.

Kenway, J., & Modra, H. (1992), Feminist pedagogy and emancipatory possibilities. In C. Luke, & J. Gore (Eds.), *Feminisms and critical pedagogy* (pp. 138–166). New York: Routledge.

Letizia, A. (2014), Radical servant leadership: A new practice of public education leadership in the post-industrial age, *Journal for Critical Education Policy Studies, 12*(2), 175–199.

Lynn, M., & Parker, L. (2006), Critical race studies in education: Examining a decade of research on U.S. Schools, *The Urban* Review, *38*(4), 257–290.

NCSL. (2018), Third grade reading legislation, National Conference of State Legislators, May 23. accessed at www.ncsl.org/research/education/thi rd-grade-reading-legislation.aspx.

Pogrow, S. (2009), Accelerate the learning of 4th and 5th graders born into poverty, *Phi Delta Kappan*, *90*, 408–412. accessed at www.eddigest.com.

Quantz, R. A., Rogers, J., & Dantley, M. (1991), Rethinking transformative leadership: Toward democratic reform of schools, *Journal of Education*, *173*(3), 96–118.

Sears, J. (1993), Responding to the sexual diversity of faculty and students: Sexual praxis and the critically reflective administrator. In C. A. Capper (Ed.), *Educational administration in a pluralistic society* (pp. 110–172). Albany, NY: State University of New York Press.

Shields, C. M. (2016), *Transformative leadership in education*, 2nd ed., New York: Routledge.

Tenet Eight
Exhibiting Moral Courage

Tenet eight of transformative leadership theory calls for moral courage. Implementing transformative leadership is not easy. Transforming an organization to be equitable, inclusive and socially just presents considerable challenges. This chapter provides support and guiding principles for acting with moral courage.

Courage is often thought to involve the kind of strength it takes to perform physical feats like some of the daring rescues we find on the news. Yet, there are also other kinds of courage, including intellectual courage, social courage, spiritual courage, and what scholars call moral courage. Courage involves, at various times, acting, not acting, speaking out, remaining silent, and asking questions. Chapter 7 of the companion volume *Transformative Leadership in Education* (Shields, 2016) provides the examples of Zahra Fasahat in Pakistan, and numerous other school leaders in the United States who exemplified moral courage in order to create equitable and inclusive schools. In this chapter, strategies for promoting moral courage are emphasized.

> Courage is what it takes to stand up and speak; courage is also what it takes to sit down and listen.
> (Winston Churchill)

When one thinks about morality, one generally thinks in terms of right and wrong, and so having moral courage is often simply defined as "doing the right thing" (Figure 8.1). However, sometimes, as will be demonstrated in this chapter, courage involves choosing between two courses of action, each of which seems right.

Figure 8.1 Do the right thing.

Some have defined moral courage more elegantly as "the alignment of outward acts with inner principles" (Kidder, 2005) or as "the behavioral expression of authenticity in the face of discomfort of dissension, disapproval, or rejection" (Francis, 2018). Each of these definitions embraces the idea that moral courage requires expression or action based on inner conviction and that it also includes the need to overcome or conquer fear as well as assess the risks involved.

To begin, identify as many people as you can (people whom you know or have heard of) who have exhibited moral courage.

Who comes to mind?

Nelson Mandela

Martin Luther King, Jr.

Gandhi

Mother Theresa

–

–

–

–

–

–

The first four were likely easy and on most people's lists. But who else did you add? Were there any people from your local community? Were there any educators? Did you remember Mary McLeod Bethune or Septima Poinsette Clark? Was your list balanced in terms of gender or race? Did it include people such as Harvey Milk, Marcia Kadish, and Tanya McCloskey, or perhaps young Avery Jackson or Malala Yousafzai? What about the fire-fighters who ran up the stairs in the World Trade Towers on September 11 instead of seeking their own safety? Did you include students from Parkland High School who, becoming activists for gun control, began by organizing a massive March for our Lives? Or Swedish student Greta Thunberg?

One of the things that this list reminds us is that moral courage is not bounded by race, nationality, sexual orientation, religion, age, or position. Yet, think about situations where moral courage seems necessary but no-one has acted. That list, for me, becomes much too long. Why did no border control agents break the rules of not touching children to offer hugs and comfort to children like the one we saw in the picture in Chapter 2? Why do guards with guns sometimes run in to stop school shooters and sometimes not? Why have so many school leaders been charged with test manipulation, with some even being sent to prison? Why do so many LBGTQ+ students indicate that teachers had seen or heard them being teased or bullied and have done nothing to stop it? Why do so many people remain silent and why does it take "whistleblowers" to report dangerous or illegal situations in industry, in government, or in non-profit organizations, including schools and universities?

Lachman developed an acronym to provide a framework for thinking about moral courage, using the word CODE, which applies to members of many professions including education (in Stokes, 2017).

Courage to be moral requires

Obligations to honor: What is the right thing to do?

Danger to manage: What do I need to handle my fear and uncertainty?

Expression and action: What action is needed to meet my obligations [...] and to maintain my integrity?

Values Required for Moral Courage

Rushworth Kidder, who has conducted numerous studies and written extensively about moral courage, suggests that there are three basic moral principles involved in developing and demonstrating moral courage. These are

- A commitment to moral *principles*
- An awareness of the *danger* involved
- A willing *endurance* of that danger

Kidder has found that no matter what group he is working with, almost everyone agrees on five key moral values that comprise the most important ethical values; these are *honesty, fairness, responsibility, respect, and compassion.* Thus, he believes it is helpful to identify, in any given difficult situation, the values at play and to determine, if several conflict, which should take priority.

What Would You Do?

Consider the following situation:

> You are a newly appointed superintendent in a small district with approximately 2000 students. You know that as a result of a financial crisis that led to the removal of the previous superintendent, the district has been in crisis and trust has been severely eroded. In fact, you are the fifth superintendent in the district in five years.
>
> After several months on the job, when you have focused on working with the board and stabilizing the financial situation, you decide it is appropriate to begin to spend time in the schools and to learn more about their culture, their strengths, and their challenges. One day, as you were walking the halls, you heard a teacher yelling at a group of kids so loudly that even though you were two hallways away, you could hear her clearly.

You know that after each school visit, when principals speak to their teachers about your visit, they blame you for any changes that need to be made. This time, you decided that it would be important for the principal to take responsibility; however, the principal was a friend and neighbor of the offending teacher and did not want to act.

As you walked, the principal shared another dilemma he was experiencing. He reported that he wanted to eliminate two counseling positions. When you ask why he might do that, he indicated that it was because the incumbent counselors were not doing their jobs adequately.

Here, there are basically two problems: 1) personnel who are failing to do their jobs (i.e., the teacher who yells at students and the counselors who are not doing their jobs); and 2) the principal who does not have the courage to address personnel issues head-on. And the principal needs to find the moral courage to address the personnel issues for the good of the students.

Assume you are the principal.

What values are in play?
How do they conflict?
Which must take priority?

1. Assessing the moral principles involved, you, as principal, have a *responsibility* to ensure a safe and welcoming learning environment for every student and hence, that the yelling must be addressed. Otherwise, you are failing in your duty to demonstrate *respect* for all students. Similarly, it is your responsibility to see that every school has counselors who are effective and supportive of students.

   You also have a duty to be *honest* with the yelling teacher, although your *compassion* for her, based on your knowledge of some personal stress she is under, seems to justify your reluctance to act. Likewise, you have a *responsibility* to enter into conversations with the counselors about your expectations and their failure to fulfill their jobs adequately. You must develop an approach for moving on but eliminating positions in order to avoid difficult conversations is simply cowardly and unacceptable.

2. As superintendent, considering the *danger* involved, you might risk pushback from the principal, teacher, and counselors, and perhaps discipline from the board if you are perceived to act too harshly, although you believe that your newly established relationship with the board is quite solid. The principal, on the other hand, risks the possible displeasure of the superintendent if he fails to act and also tensions in his relationship with the teacher and counselors if he does. There may also be a danger of divided community backing for these educators.

3. Both seem willing to *endure* the discomfort and risks of maintaining their stand. Here the question is which of the values has priority. Is *responsibility* to ensure a respectful learning environment for the students more important or is it *compassion* for the individual teacher and counselors? What is *fair* for the students? These are the kinds of questions that may be asked whenever an ethical dilemma presents itself.

   Here, it seems obvious that teachers should not be screaming at students, and that counsellors should be doing their jobs, and hence that, in each case, the behavior must be addressed by the principal as part of his responsibilities. Moreover, given that the superintendent has asked for action, the risks seem relatively minimal. In other situations, however, the suitable courses of action may be less obvious.

Getting Started

In any difficult situation, an excellent starting point is to use the following checklist adapted from Kidder's (1995) work:

- Evaluate the circumstances to establish whether moral courage is needed in the situation.
- Determine what moral values and ethical principles are at risk or in question of being compromised.
- Ascertain what principles need to be expressed and defended in the situation—focus on one or two of the more critical values.

- Consider the possible adverse consequences/risks associated with taking action.
- Assess whether or not the adversity can be endured—determine what support/resources are available.
- Avoid stumbling blocks that might restrain moral courage, such as apprehension or over-reflection leading to reasoning oneself out of being morally courageous in the situation.
- Continue to develop moral courage through education, training, and practice.

RESOURCES You may find it useful to download the template, *"Developing moral courage,"* based on these questions, found in the eResources.

Start Small

One way to continue to develop *moral courage* is to "start small." In other words, you should practice what you preach in the small decisions you make every day. If your restaurant bill has omitted a charge for something, tell the server. If you have forgotten to complete a report on time, own up to it rather than making an excuse. If you have said something inappropriate to someone, apologize.

Know Yourself

RESOURCES To begin to prepare for exercising moral courage, it is useful, as indicated in Chapter 1, to really know yourself. There you were asked to identify your non-negotiables. Here, additional questions have been added.

Know Yourself

What are your non-negotiables?
What are your strengths? Your weaknesses?
What are your greatest fears?
Where do these fears come from?

One common fear is worrying about what others will think—a fear that rarely brings more than temporary and minimal consequences. Thus, it is also useful to ask, as Socrates did to Crito, "Why do we care so much about the opinions of others?"

If you are concerned that taking an unpopular stand will affect your job security or inhibit opportunities for advancement, it is important to ask whether the fear is real or imagined. Are you afraid because you know someone who was negatively affected? Have you read about a similar situation ending badly? How can you muster support and resources to avoid this same outcome?

Prepare in Advance

Some experts suggest that, in addition to analyzing the situation using the aforementioned strategies, it may be useful to engage in what is called "cognitive reframing" and to ask oneself what if the worst thing you can think of actually happens. What would you do then?

Learn from "Failure"

The foregoing "preparation" is useful for situations in which you have time to reflect on your options and make an informed decision. However, often, one is called to respond to a situation on the spot. Educators often overhear teachers or students talking disparagingly, teasing, or making jokes at another's expense.

What Would You Do?

In one school, students began to report to the principal and their teachers that they were hearing racist and homophobic jokes and that no-one seemed to be aware of the situation. The superintendent then asked that all students be surveyed to determine how they defined racism, sexism, or homophobia and to indicate whether they had seen evidence of these negative practices in the school. Students wrote candidly, indicating they had heard many comments including:

- I've been sexually harassed by a boy during lunch a couple of years ago where a boy did unwelcome verbal and physical things to me while my friends sat there arguing and I ended up laughing to hold back my tears.
- Jokes that I've heard: how many Mexicans does it take to jump the border? Tres because there is no tres-passing. You are from Germany; well the holocaust is definitely for you.
- Kids say this joke. What is something that is black and yellow and screams? ... a bus filled with black people falling off a cliff.

When educators were asked to indicate how they might respond if they overheard such comments, most were at a loss. Many indicated they would tell students that such statements were hurtful or ask why they wanted to hurt other people. Some felt it was simply a function of kids being kids and that no harm was really meant or done.

How would you respond if you saw or heard these situations?

At the time, you, too, might be stymied about how to respond. But if you hear a comment like these on one occasion, it is important that you prepare yourself for the next one. Failure to respond on one occasion is not necessarily a lack of moral courage, but perhaps a lack of knowledge (although if that is the case, it is essential to follow up later). However, if you do not take the time to reflect and to consider what a possible good response might have been, and if the situation continues to repeat itself, that is a different situation altogether and it might well be possible to consider that you have lacked moral courage.

For Reflection

How can I communicate a non-judgmental explanation of behavior that needs to be changed?

Have I used an "I" statement to communicate how I feel? E.g., When you tell a joke like that, I feel … ."

Have I explained how telling that joke might affect someone else?

Have I clearly explained what behavior solution I am asking for?

Would it be sufficient to simply ask a student who told the joke about the bus why he or she wanted to hurt others? Can your response be adequate if it does not address the blatant racism of the "joke"? In what ways can the racism be addressed? These are the kinds of questions you might ask teachers to write about, share, discuss, and even role play as a way of learning from a lack of adequate response in the beginning.

 ## Moving Forward

Starratt (1991), a well-known scholar of educational leadership, wrote about the need to exhibit the three ethics of justice, critique, and care, to which some add the concept of community. And in any given difficult situation, it may be useful to ask how each of these may be exhibited. In the foregoing situation, overhearing students telling jokes, *justice* may be demonstrated by addressing the racism as well as the harm with the perpetrator. *Critique*, as we saw in the previous chapter, might involve ensuring that students and teachers understand and can explain the issues inherent in the situation. *Care* involves addressing the outcomes for both the perpetrator and the student(s) to whom the comments were addressed, including an understanding of their relationships and emotional responses. And finally, *community* requires that the conversations are generalized and extend to developing both empathy and understanding on the part of everyone, and not just those who overheard the initial exchange.

Other Strategies for Developing Moral Courage

There are numerous strategies suggested in the literature that will help to develop and consolidate moral courage. Here I suggest only a few.

Build Safety Nets and Then Let Go

There is an amazing YouTube video that combines an exciting circus trapeze performance of 1950 with the reading of an excerpt called *The Parable of the Trapeze* read by Danaan Parry (2009) and taken from his book *Warriors of the Heart* 🔗. It demonstrates visually that, as the words state:

> Sometimes, I feel that my life is a series of trapeze swings. I'm either hanging on to a trapeze bar swinging along or, for a few moments, I'm hurtling across space between the trapeze bars.
>
> Mostly, I spend my time hanging on for dear life to the trapeze bar of the moment. [...] But once in a while, as I'm merrily, or not so merrily, swinging along, I look ahead of me into the distance, and what do I see?
>
> I see another trapeze bar looking at me. It's empty. And I know, in that place in me that knows, that this new bar has my name on it. It is my next step, my growth, my aliveness coming to get me. In my heart of hearts, I know that for me to grow, I must release my grip on the present well-known bar to move to the new one.

Perry goes on to suggest that despite successful releases in the past, each time we have to let go, perhaps filled with terror; and sometimes, in fact, we do fall. However, there is still a safety net, and as we climb up to begin again, we may realize we have actually learned to fly.

Build Trust

This section presents some ways of developing trust—trust in yourself and in your peers as safety nets for reaching out, letting go, and flying across the abyss to take the next courageous stance. Some strategies for fortifying yourself include:

1. **Journaling**. In previous chapters, I have suggested the utility of having people write and reflect. To develop moral courage, asking people to keep a journal of microaggressions they witness or of critical moral dilemmas and their preferred course of action is an excellent activity.

2. **Share moral examples.** I recently watched, with tears in my eyes, the story of a young Black woman, Starr Carter, depicted in the powerful movie adaptation, *The Hate U Give*. Starr was the only witness to the death of her unarmed friend as he was shot by a police officer and ultimately had to decide in whom she could confide and find the courage to take a stand—even if it meant putting herself and her family at risk. Watching or reading about acts of courage and engaging in follow-up discussion can help to strengthen others' resolve to act courageously. Other movies such as *Schindler's List* or *The Blind Side* also come to mind.

3. **Read and discuss fiction**. Winner of numerous awards for literature, Ann Holm's 1963 novel, *I am David*, is an inspiring story of a young boy who, with the help of a prison guard, escapes from a concentration camp and travels across Europe, learning many lessons along the way. Fictional stories of courage may be used to discuss courage with children as well as with educators who are learning to take a courageous stand. Others that come to mind include the novels of Catherine Ryan Hyde such as *Pay it Forward* or Baca's *A Place to Stand* (although the latter would not be appropriate to use with young students).

> Develop your own list of books and movies that are appropriate for adults and students of various ages and that exemplify moral courage.

4. **Build Community.** In the parable of the trapeze, there are several flying trapeze artists who demonstrate trust in one another, demonstrating once again that the more you have a community that will support and fortify you as you determine to act courageously, the better off

you are. Sometimes, though, taking the most courageous action is not a single decision of one person, but requires the agreement of the group to move forward in an honest and courageous way. Here, you may find yourself in need of negotiating a suitable, ethical, and equitable course of action.

5. **Think Together. Seek Consensus.** I find the discussion of consensus by Wynn and Guditus (1984) to be helpful. They remind us that the word consensus originally meant "to think together," and that it does not necessarily imply total agreement. In fact, as they admit, often unanimous agreement is not possible. Thus, a process must be found that involves "reaching agreement to implement a decision that appears to be most acceptable to the group as a whole" (p. 43). They describe it in the following way:

> Consensus must be preceded by an experience of "thinking together," which includes taking all members' needs into consideration, listening to and understanding dissenters' views, attempting to reconcile conflicting goals, striving for solutions that accommodate opposing views, and securing the commitment to implement the decision even from those members who would have preferred another solution.
>
> (p. 43)

Before beginning to "think together," it may be useful to decide on some ground rules, including the meaning of consensus.

First, recall the importance of hearing all voices and ask yourself which voices have been heard and whose have been silenced. As the definition of Wynn and Guditus indicates, it is important to ensure that everyone has had an opportunity to speak their truth. However, given it is rare to find complete agreement, and that it is easy to find the group "spinning its wheels" and going over and over the same material, when everyone has had the opportunity to speak, and there are still one or two hold-outs, you may have to invoke the agreed-upon definition of consensus and ask questions like:

- Have all perspectives been heard?
- Is there any new information we need to have?
- Do we have enough agreement to move forward?

- Do you feel you have been understood?
- Is there something you feel has not been heard or understood about your perspective?
- Are you willing to let go of your position in order to permit the group to move forward?

The process of thinking together, of assuring that everyone's voice has been heard, and of finding creative solutions that incorporate the basic objectives but that permit the group to move forward, is a very useful way of thinking about consensus.

> Seeking consensus does not involve voting, even when full acceptance is not readily achieved.
>
> (Wynn & Guditus, p. 48)

6. **Learn to Negotiate.** A related process is that of negotiation which also may require moral courage.

A Process for Negotiating

Ask for others' preferred courses of action.

Together, identify the ways in which each course of action fulfills the criteria of being honest, fair, responsible, respectful, and compassionate.

Identify your preferred course of action and explain why.

Jointly decide on the best course of action.

If there is not total agreement, you may have to ask some of the following questions related to consensus in order to move the group forward.

Do you feel you have been understood?

Is there something you feel has not been heard or understood about your perspective?

Are you willing to let go of your minority position in order to permit the group to move forward?

Is there a compromise you can identify that you find satisfactory but that still meets our basic objectives?

7. **Share Narratives of Identity.** One strategy that is extremely powerful is to ask people at a meeting to share what I have come to call "narratives of identity." I first used this technique when attending a conference with several doctoral students who wanted to share their stories of identity including some experiences of marginalization and oppression.

An Example

One told how at his birth his White mother was told he had jaundice and would need to remain in the hospital. Only when his African American father arrived to see his son, did the hospital staff recognize that his skin color was due to his mixed race and not to any medical situation that might be "corrected."

Another spoke of his arrival as a refugee, having been part of the expulsion of Asians from Uganda by Idi Amin during the 1970s, and how much he had suffered by being poor and lacking knowledge of western culture and customs.

A third spoke about some of the challenges growing up as a "preachers' kid" and wanting to both comply with the dictates of his parents and to fit in with his peers.

As I thought about my contribution, I began to try to recall a time when I, too, had been marginalized. However, my examples were trivial and temporary, based on receiving the top grades in a class, or not being very athletic. As I reflected, I realized that an honest sharing of my situation required that I name the privilege into which I had been born and from which I benefit on an ongoing basis. At the same time, I acknowledged that having privilege does not spare you from pain and also shared some of the details of a very difficult divorce I had gone through a few years before.

The experience of sharing was in itself powerful and helped to bolster my courage to speak more often about my personal experiences but what was particularly surprising was that a number of colleagues from the audience approached each of us with tears in their eyes, saying they had never had the courage to share similar experiences. Even more surprising was that the following year, at the annual conference, several of these same colleagues came to us reporting some of the positive experiences they had had during the year as they developed the courage to become more authentic by sharing their own personal stories with colleagues and students. Honesty and vulnerability invite others to become vulnerable and to share their experiences as well.

Assessing Progress

How does one assess the development of moral courage? Being courageous is not simply a matter of having values, but requires the ability to *act* on values. It also requires us to recognize that, as Maya Angelou once stated:

> In diversity there is beauty and there is strength. We all should know that diversity makes for a rich tapestry, and we must understand that all the threads of that tapestry are equal in value no matter their color.

If, as part of accepting the mandate for change described in Chapter 1, you have conducted an audit of the school climate and included a listing of the kinds and frequencies of "jokes" that represent prejudice, or of microaggressions, or comments reflecting deficit thinking, then you have a baseline against which to measure your progress. Conduct a follow-up audit to identify areas of progress as well as areas which still require effort. Create a "courage" wall in the staffroom and ask people to share times when they feel they spoke up, stood with or for others, or took action that represented moral courage. You may be surprised at how many incidents people are willing to share.

Concluding Thoughts

Although exhibiting moral courage is a necessary part of being a transformative leader, it is not easy. Making change that equalizes the playing field is always perceived as "taking something away" from one person or group and favoring another. There will be push back. There will be disagreement. There will be periodic hostility. There will be some—particularly those with power—who feel threatened by the redistribution of power and privilege, by the democratization of resources and pedagogies and by the creation of more inclusive and equitable institutions. Nevertheless, transformation must occur. This is where an assessment of your ability to endure becomes critical. It may be useful if you memorize and repeat, as a kind of mantra, or post for inspiration, some of the following statements about the need for courage that have come to us across time. The authors include some whose names we know and some we may not, but all of them express the need for, and the power of, courage.

> The world is a dangerous place, not because of those who do evil, but because of those who look on and do nothing.
>
> (Einstein)

> To see what is right and not to do it is want of courage.
>
> (Confucius)

> A ship is safe in harbor, but that's not what ships are for.
>
> (John A. Shedd)

> Courage was not the absence of fear, but the triumph over it. The brave man is not he who does not feel afraid, but he who conquers that fear.
>
> (Nelson Mandela)

> Courage isn't having the strength to go on - it is going on when you don't have strength.
>
> (Napoleon Bonaparte)

> If you want to rebel, rebel from inside the system. That's much more powerful than rebelling outside the system.
>
> (Marie Lu)

> Risk anything! Care no more for the opinion of others ... Do the hardest thing on earth for you. Act for yourself. Face the truth.
>
> (Katherine Mansfield)

Perhaps most importantly, activist, CEO, and marking analyst, Jon Mertz links the need for moral courage with good leadership, saying, "Moral courage empowers good leadership, and it challenges and, potentially, prevents bad leadership." The need is urgent. Until we transform our education systems – from kindergarten through high school to higher education – to be more

> Moral courage empowers good leadership, and it challenges and, potentially, prevents bad leadership.
>
> Jon Mertz, 2018

equitable, inclusive, and socially just, we will fail to realize the promise of education as a powerful weapon to change the world. Instead, civil unrest will continue to challenge the well-being of our democratic society.

In the next chapter, you will find the first-person reflections and experiences of a courageous and committed, young school principal who developed and implanted a plan for a turnaround school that re-opened in the fall of 2018, based specifically and explicitly on the principles of transformative leadership theory. There she shares her journey of moral courage, her approach, her challenges, and her successes in order to support others who are embarking on similar journeys of transforming educational institutions where they are.

References

Francis, S. L. (2018), *The courage way: Leading and living with integrity.* San Francisco, CA: Berrett-Koehler.

Kidder, R. (1995), *How good people make tough choices: Resolving the dilemmas of ethical living.* New York: HarperCollins.

Kidder, R. (2005), *Moral courage.* New York: HarperCollins.

Mertz, J. (2018), Moral courage: What is our leadership responsibility? Thin difference. accessed April, 2019 at www.thindifference.com/2018/05/moral-courage-leadership-responsibility/.

Parry, D. (2009), *Warriors of the heart.* Bellingham, WA: The Earthstewards Network.

Shields, C. M. (2016), *Transformative leadership in education*, 2nd ed., New York: Routledge.

Starratt, R. J. (1991), Building an ethical school: A theory for practice in educational leadership, *Educational Administration Quarterly, 27*(2), 185–202.

Stokes, L. (2017), Learn how to cultivate moral courage, *Healthy Nurse, Healthy Nation.* accessed at https://engage.healthynursehealthynation .org/blogs/8/685.

Wynn, R., & Guditus, C. W. (1984), *Team management: Leadership by consensus.* New York: McGraw-Hill.

A Voice from the Field

Angelina M. Walker

> **Note:** In this chapter, we hear the voice of a courageous transformative school leader who followed the tenets of transformative leadership to create a new school. Here, we learn more about her efforts, her challenges, and her plans to move forward.[1]

> I raise up my voice—not so I can shout but so that those without a voice can be heard … we cannot succeed when half of us are held back.
>
> (Malala)

I didn't always know myself. Well, not in the way that one would perceive me today. One would say that the journey to know myself as a leader and understand my moral purpose and compass was a not a single road traveled but rather a path of interconnected streams, rivers, valleys, streets, dirt roads, back alleyways, and highways. To know me and my moral purpose in education and life is to know my life story. To develop yours, is to authentically know your story and moral purpose as well.

My Journey

I was born to an Italian mother and Black father in the 1980s in the heart of Denver, Colorado. I was the only child, although later I would have two siblings that did not make it full term and a sister through the adoption of my cousin whose parents were in and out of jail. During this time, Denver was seeing an influx of gangs in the metro area, coming east from Los Angeles. My neighborhood was a combination of working class, Black families, struggling to survive and the LA gangs making a name for themselves there. It was a beautiful mixture of pride, heritage, pain, and struggle.

My mother was the only White woman in the neighborhood. She taught me what it meant to be a strong, biracial woman who advocates for what is morally right. She saw first-hand the pain and plight of our community, knew her privilege, and walked hand-in-hand with all around her, to make a better life for myself and the children in our neighborhood. She attended community meetings where she shared her voice to ensure the safety of the kids in our 'hood. Our house was a gathering spot for all 'E-block' kids and many star-filled nights would be spent playing Old Lady Witch across green lawns, hiding amongst prickly bushes, and capturing gleaming fireflies that lit up the night sky.

My mother sent me to an all-Black preschool and kindergarten from two years old to five, run by a fiercely strong Black woman who was a deeply rooted educational activist. Here is where I learned about pride and culturally responsive education: we sang the Black National Anthem at all school events, we learned about *our* history, and we got to personally know many Black leaders in our community as part of our legacy projects. We volunteered in senior living homes and were pushed to the highest of expectations for reading and math, taught that this was the path to self and community freedom. All of us who attended the school, which was an old home converted into a two-room schoolhouse, located right behind my backyard, understood the value of education in our Black community, and all of us left above grade level in reading and math.

This was the beginning of my understanding of who I was and the *development of my moral courage*. My early years were spent evolving into a strong, future leader. It is where I first learned about rooting all things in love, respect, and unity.

During my teenage and college years, I learned about the importance of leadership and equity. I attended a very large metropolitan comprehensive high school with over 2000 students. This high school was the definition of an oxymoron. Situated in the heart of Denver, coming from the east were the very rich White students, who lived in Hilltop. They were the students of parents who were doctors, lawyers, and politicians. Coming from the north were the Black, Brown, and Indigenous students from North Hilltop. They were the students of working-class families, struggling to survive. The school was very much divided by color as well. If you could draw a line down the middle of the school, you would be able to visibly see the color of students from Hilltop and North Hilltop. You would know that all of the Black students hung out at the church (right next to the school) to play basketball or on the South Lawn during lunch. You would know that the White students left in their BMWs and Benzes to eat off campus at Chipotle or Starbucks. You would know that the X classes (short for accelerated) and advanced placement (AP) classes were for White students and the "regular" classes were for others.

When I first started at this high school, I was on the X Track. I was taking advanced classes. After one particularly trying semester, in which I received a C in a science class, my counselor told me I needed to get into regular classes and that the X Track would no longer be available to me, thus cutting off AP offerings for me. The first day I stepped into a "regular" literature class, I understood why I was sent there. Everyone looked like me. Going from being one of the only students of color in my X Class to having no White students in the regular class shook me to my core.

I began to ponder the role of education in communities of color and I realized how one could slip through the cracks of public education. I began to examine the inequities in my school, which would later lead to my leadership development in college and education. I had always wanted to be a teacher, but now I wanted to become an educator who changed practice, policy, and systems.

All of my combined experiences helped me develop my strong sense of moral purpose, a necessity in becoming a transformative leader. So who am I? Mother. Lover. Italian and Black. Educator. Doctor. Principal. Warrior. Researcher on race, equity, social justice, and educational leadership. Artist. Denver native. Truth speaker and seeker. Bold. Aware. Aspiring to be enlightened. I believe in love, respect, unity, leadership, and equity. These pull my strong moral compass.

A Transformative Educator

I am an observer. I am not the typical dominant leader. I am conscientious and constantly reflecting. I prefer to pause and think before jumping to decisions, and I have learned to ask for time for that personal reflection from my colleagues and peers. I collaborate, knowing that I need multiple perspectives in order to fully understand a situation. I always ask whose voice is missing from the table and pursue ways to garner that voice. I strongly believe in sharing narratives of identity in order to produce change and I believe in learning from the past in order to initiate that change. I believe in questions, asking lots of questions, and I believe in failure, because it is important to be humble enough to accept when things are not going right in order to change them and yourself for the better. Truly knowing myself was the most important step in **accepting my personal mandate for deep and equitable change**.

In the Spring of 2017, I was granted the opportunity to begin on my path of changing practice, policy, and systems in public education, and to **focus on democracy, emancipation, equity and justice**. I was asked to become the principal of a turnaround elementary school (three years old through fifth grade), a school that was deemed in need of severe intervention. The school and community were forced to vote on a new program with a new plan, new leadership, and new staff. As the leader of the turnaround school, I would be given a year of planning time prior to opening the doors in the fall of 2018. Throughout the planning process and first year of the school, I collaboratively developed a plan that had multiple strengths and multiple learning opportunities. The path toward transformative practice is not a straight arrow, but has multiple twists and turns, with multiple highs and lows.

From the initial stages of planning, I understood the importance of taking risks, maintaining the vision and mission of the school, examining areas of equity and inequity, and building strong community alliances and safety nets in the form of true perspective-seeking and collaboration. From the early days of planning for the school, I met with the staff of the previous school that was closing down. Many of the staff supported in writing the new plan for the school. We spent countless hours in the library learning from our strengths and discussing next steps. I also worked with the families of the school closing down to ensure that their voices were heard. Throughout the process, hundreds of family members were brought in front of the school board to share their desire for a solid education and a small community-based school in the heart of our neighborhood. I met with multiple members of the community, everyone from local law enforcement, to pastors, to single-mothers in their homes, in order to understand what they wanted for the education of their children. Through understanding of our *interconnectedness, interdependence, and global awareness*, their ideas developed as a basis for the school plan.

Hiring

My first goal within the plan was to hire a team that matched the demographics of our students. This was no easy task as the demographics of the school are 99% students of color (with 76% being of Latinx descent, 13% Black, and 1% other). 62% of our students were bilingual with Spanish as their first language, and 95% were students eligible for free and reduced-price lunch. With the current trend in education being that 78% of teachers are White females, I knew that this would be difficult systemically. I attended multiple recruitment fairs and changed the hiring process to include questions about race and equity. I used questions about values and the history of our country as pre-questions to screen applicants during hiring fairs. I individually met with each candidate and completed a values-based phone or in-person screen. Each face-to-face interview required a successful pre-screen, a video or in-person sample lesson, a lesson plan submission, and a written component, in addition to the face-to-face interview. If successful after the in-person interview, then a walk-through of the school was scheduled to see if the educator felt that the school was a family that they wanted to become a part of. Through our hiring plan, we were able to secure 68% teachers of color (89% staff of color including paraprofessionals, secretaries, lunch, and custodial services), 50% educators from the community we were serving, 52% bilingual, and 20% male educators. Although we did not match the actual demographics of the school, we are able to confidently say that we were making progress toward a more equitable learning environment where the educators mirrored our students and community. In fact, we are one of the top schools in Denver with regards to hiring faculty of color.

Community Building

My next step was to ensure that enrollment did not drop during our initial year. This meant a lot of community and trust building. It meant showing my face during the planning year at all school events for the school that was closing down. It meant countless hours of community forums with tough questions being asked, and being open to the vulnerability and realness in answering those tough questions. It meant home visits and barbeques in the park. It meant apologizing for historical wrongs that had happened to the school and community. It meant being able to articulate a plan and vision for the school that was based in the community's hopes and desires.

Unfortunately, what also comes with turnaround is the rebranding of the identity of the school. Since the previous school was a pillar within the community (I, myself, had played multiple times at the school park when I was growing up) and had been established for decades prior, it was important for me to make sure that the rebranding of the school did not impact the community in a detrimental way. I knew some rebranding was necessary, in order to show that we were coming in stronger than ever, but I did not want to lose the sense of family that had been built previously. Through community feedback, we decided to keep the name of the school, the mascot, and colors and provide the option to utilize the same uniforms that had been available years prior. Many students were using hand-me-downs from older siblings and it was important for families to have a financially sustainable option. We brought back the middle initial of the namesake of the school (which was the original school's name) and offered other options of uniforms. We took the mascot and made it twenty-first century in look and feel. We established ourselves as part of a small network of public schools in our community and branded with the hashtag #happykidslearnmore.

During the first year of the school, I invited several members of the community in to speak to our staff about the history and legacy of the neighborhood and how turnaround has impacted them personally and education within our community. Unfortunately, in our neighborhood, turnaround has forced the only comprehensive high school to close down and most elementary and middle schools were shut down in an effort to "make schools better." What popped up in place were turnaround schools that were semi-effective at best and ineffective at worst. This acknowledgment to the community, that I saw their pain and hurt and that I was unfortunately a part of the system of turnaround, had to be recognized. Part of coming in as a turnaround principal meant that I would have to acknowledge the very real pains of turnaround in my community, while simultaneously participating in and helping to change the devastating effects of the turnaround process.

Creating Equitable Systems

All of this allowed me not only to develop more equitable systems within our school, but also to develop community, a core tenet of transformative leadership. The purpose to build community is to **redistribute power in more equitable ways**, to seek multiple perspectives, and to learn from the mistakes of the past in order to generate a better future for kids and community. Understanding our community's context—social, political, and cultural—was a core action that was and continues to be a priority today.

During the initial planning stages, I also constantly referenced the teaching of several critical theories in order to reflect on, assess, and critique multiple aspects of our educational culture that we were building including critical race theory, critical queer studies, and critical feminist theories, just to name a few. I also examined the foundations of transformative leadership theory, which is the crux of who I am as a leader. It was important for me to ground myself in who I was as a leader—equitable, inclusive, excellent, and socially just—in order to be able to name injustice and develop policy and practice that addressed it. It was also important for myself to identify my biases in order to combat them. I held some deeply seated beliefs around education, due to my experiences growing up or that were embedded throughout formal education training, which needed to be and were challenged, such as sitting in rows, discipline policies, and teaching practices in general.

As we stepped into the new school year, my first priority was to instill in my staff a love for our vision, mission, and purpose and to **challenge previous mindsets**. As our mission states, "Together, we ensure all learners achieve excellence in academics and the arts, while simultaneously empowering kids, families, and staff in our community as diverse and equitable changemakers." It was important to begin the year with this staff vision setting, team building, trust making, and honest data analysis. We did this through countless activities built on equity and our purpose and mission. We made collaborative quilts and honored our educators as the bones of our community family. We grew, bonded, and released feelings together. We broke bread together. We added additional time for culturally responsive practice analysis and dialogue. We modified our calendar to fit the needs of our community. We analyzed data and co-planned with our network school down the street. We built each other up.

During the school year, we **balanced public and private good** by providing continuous support and guidance through weekly observation and feedback sessions run by teacher leaders, who were still part-time in the classroom. We analyzed our data to examine our disproportionalities. We rooted our conversations in being brave and courageous, calling out inequities as we saw them. We incorporated culturally responsive learning block times and trauma-informed practices. We held discussions and conversations on academic high expectations for all students in the building.

We *redistributed power* for families and students. We created spaces for families to feel welcome and valued, whether that was through monthly snack and chats, the School Advisory Board, community forums, home visits, partnering with local community supports, or hosting monthly celebrations of students, achievement, and culture. We were number one in our district for the number of home visits completed and our School Advisory Board was run bilingually by a community leader. We utilized social media and numerous news outlets to highlight the wonders of our school community.

During our first year we also took on school-wide restorative practices. We created a "TABS" room that our kids could utilize themselves to "take a break." In this room, students set a timer and walked through a series of tasks to calm and refocus themselves including identifying how they felt, using sensory objects, trampolines, bouncy balls, calming lights, coloring, and music. We taught teachers how to conduct restorative conversations and hired a team of socio-emotional supports including a nurse, psychologist, social worker, two restorative practices coordinators, and a socio-emotional senior team lead. We continued some of the positive behavior support traditions that were in place including the earning of scholar dollars, provided to all students when they demonstrated our core values. During the Christmas season, which most of our students celebrate, we hosted a gift-buying celebration. Teachers and staff donated items and put them on display. Every student in the school got to use their scholar dollars to "purchase" and wrap items for their loved ones to give them at Christmas time. My own son bought me a coffee mug, and proudly gave it to me on Christmas day. To this day, it is still the coffee mug that I use daily.

We established community partnerships such as partnering with a local church to provide a bag of food every other week to each student in our school, at no cost. We worked with local high-school students to have weekly volunteer reading sessions and we brought in local groups for science and culture nights.

Teachers and administrators hung posters in offices and around the school building celebrating Black lives, Indigenous cultures, the LGBTQAI, community and many more. Student work was displayed with the standards and an opportunity for other students and teachers to provide feedback. We established clear expectations for rigor and high expectations. We developed classroom walkthrough sheets that were based in culturally responsive practices.

Challenges

However, the year was not always successful. Unfortunately, we came to a quick realization that hardly anything that you plan for on paper fulfills in the same way as you hoped and that merely documenting the inequities that were present was not enough in itself to change schools into equitable places. As the school leader, I quickly learned that our students had a lot of socio-emotional needs and although our hope was that every student would come to school completely happy and be successful in our class-rooms, the fact of the matter was that they were not. We were not immune to outbursts, walking out of class, teachers engaging in power struggles, and feelings, at times, of hopelessness. We had to modify, and remodify, again and again and again, our plans.

We had to call each other out in times of injustice. For example, on one particular day, after looking at the discipline data and noticing a trend of phone calls to the front office for Black boys (98% of calls and referrals for Saturday restoration were for Black boys), I presented the data to the staff, calling out the inequities and having a courageous and difficult conversation with my leadership team.

We noticed that although we did a great job initiating restorative practices, teachers were not equipped with the skills to conduct them themselves. We noticed that in times of stress, our own school leaders would revert to traditional discipline practices.

Teachers were not able to deeply analyze standards without intense leadership support and unfortunately we often heard language used that was not equitable, including, "They can't do it!" when referring to students' academic abilities. Because so much focus was placed on culture during the first year, unfortunately our instruction and individual teacher support suffered.

In terms of myself as a leader, I personally made some assumptions about where my staff were along the culturally responsive continuum. I didn't take into account espoused beliefs versus lived actions, and unfortunately, our students and community did suffer. However, part of the growth of a transformative leader is to acknowledge where you currently are in order to right your wrongs.

Moving Forward

Here, knowing the realities of the school, it is important to **balance the critique of our systems with the promise of hope and possibility for future action**. I recognize and hope you do too that exercising transformative leadership is not, nor will it ever be, easy. However, my priority as a transformative leader is to understand and acknowledge our shortcomings, while simultaneously driving the hope, possibility, and future action that is needed to create equitable change. Moving forward some immediate next steps include:

- Supporting teachers not just with the theory of restorative practices but the how of restorative practices
- Providing more culturally responsive training for working with students of color, especially Black boys
- Thinking outside of the box: how to take traditional discipline practices and make them culturally responsive, equitable, restorative, and socially just
- Using deep standards analysis during planning and weekly data team meetings
- Shifting language to that of high expectations and belief in our kids
- Downsizing the administrative team in order to reprioritize and place more support directly in front of students, with a focus on instruction
- Maintaining the culture that we have begun building and continuously shouting out and remembering all of the good we are doing
- Making sure that lesson plans are relevant and engaging
- Ensuring that students are actively engaged in questioning and sense-making activities
- Making sure that all are on board with our mission and vision and providing students the opportunity to access educational standards and curriculum on their own—recognizing that this is an act of equity in and of itself
- Focusing on the opportunity gap present in our school.

Concluding Reflections

These next steps will require a lot of honesty and vulnerability. As mentioned before, the work of transformative leadership is never done, and is never easy. My hope is that my educational system, the parts that I directly impact, will evolve into more healthy, equitable, loving, inclusive systems and that I will continue to be a constant voice for equity and change, in terms of policy, practice, and ideology. It is easy to give up and to give into larger influences and systems that support the status quo. However, although we still have our challenges we face, I will not be silenced into submission. Instead, my hope is that through this honest reflection, I will continue to use my leadership and voice to advocate for, and ultimately influence, educational change.

Here are some questions for you to use in your personal reflection and action planning. As mentioned previously, reflection is an important tool for recognizing where you have come from, where you are, and where you are planning to go

For Reflection

1. Think about the history of and interconnectedness between your values and morals. **How do you, as a transformative leader, infuse your values and morals into your daily work and interactions?**

    Some actionable ideas include: ensuring that the mission, vision, and values mention equity; including equity in your daily calendar—if it's a priority, it's in your calendar; common values language.

2. Think about who has the power and makes the decisions regarding the systems, policies, and practices within your building. **How do you, as a transformative leader, redistribute that power to ensure all around the table have equitable opportunity and voice in decision making?**

    Some actionable ideas include: hiring process that includes questions about equity; decision-making models that support multiple perspectives and voices; intentional recruitment from all voices to participate in decision-making groups for the school.

3. Think about the staff in your building: your teachers, custodial crew, lunchroom managers, secretaries, etc. **How can you, as a transformative leader, shift mindsets that do not align with values and equitable practices, policies, and systems?**

    Some actionable ideas include: professional development tied to mind-shift changes; team-building exercises; community walks and talks.

4. Think about the instruction, curriculum, learning environment, and learning opportunities within your building. **How do you, as a transformative leader, support a learning movement that promotes all students achieving at high levels?**

    Some actionable ideas include: clear expectations for student democracy, agency and participation within classrooms; learning opportunities that include global awareness and cultural interconnectedness; environments and learning opportunities that support the whole child.

5. Think about how your current policies, practices, and systems are equitable and inequitable. **What actions, as a transformative leader, must you implement in order to ensure that your policies, practices, and systems are equitable for all?**

    Some actionable ideas include: intense data analysis; reflection circles with feedback; action planning with administration, teachers, families, students.

Note

1 To cite this chapter please use the following: Walker, A. M. (2019), A voice from the field, in Shields, C. M., *Becoming a transformative leader: A guide to creating equitable schools*, New York, Routledge, Ch. 10.

10 | Transformation Begins

This chapter reiterates the need for, and the benefits of, transformative leadership theory and presents some concluding thoughts and, hopefully, some encouragement for moving forward.

In the previous nine chapters, we have provided some thoughts and starting points for becoming a transformative leader and for creating equitable, inclusive, excellent, and socially just schools.

You will know, based on the detailed discussion of the eight tenets and of Dr. Angelina M. Walker's first-hand experience, that being a transformative leader is not easy. There are no prescriptions, no set of eight or ten steps one can follow, and no detailed roadmap for creating an equitable school. But there are guiding principles or tenets and some key questions that can inform leadership practice and decision making. At the same time, unless and until school leaders adopt a mindset of equity, inclusion, and social justice, and find, within themselves, a considerable amount of moral courage, schools will continue to privilege some students and marginalize others. And the gaps of achievement, opportunity, and empowerment will not close.

If you have also read the original book to which this is a companion, *Transformative Leadership in Education* (Shields, 2016), you will know that in the concluding chapters there are examples of morally courageous transformative leaders. Because they were at different stages of their journeys and worked in different contexts, their actions and their starting points were different; however, they provide some ideas for getting started. The goal of this book was to offer additional strategies, activities, and ideas to use during the implementation of transformative leadership theory in any educational institution. Regardless of how unsure you feel, it is important to keep in mind both the need for transformative leadership and the eight tenets we have discussed that work as an integral and interconnected whole.

Summarizing the Need for Transformative Leadership

We have repeatedly asserted that in America (and in most other developed countries) there are huge educational disparities between those students from the dominant culture and language and others. Those from non-dominant cultures in general[1] drop out (or are pushed out) in greater numbers, fail to go on to higher education, perform less well on tests, earn less in their lifetimes, and experience greater illnesses and levels of poverty. We have also affirmed the disparities in disciplinary rates and suspensions between Black and Brown students and their White or Asian peers.

Educators do not enter the field of education to perpetuate discrimination and disparity. In fact, most educators choose their career because of a deep desire to improve the lot of all students. This was confirmed when a study from Columbia University asked teachers why they teach, despite low wages and often a lack of recognition. Their responses were consistent with the words of poet William Butler Yeats, "Education is not the filling of a pail, but the lighting of a fire," as they talked about how rewarding it is to help children realize that learning can be hard, and that it is okay." Yet, despite teachers' passions for learning and for students, the outcomes are often discouraging.

In 2017, Desilver, for the Pew Research Center, reported the results of the international academic testing program PISA in these words: "U.S. students' academic achievement still lags that of their peers in many other countries." The article cited the most recent available PISA results, from 2015, which placed the United States "an unimpressive 38th out of 71 countries in math and 24th in science." Desilver also cited the 2015 National Assessment of Educational Progress (NAEP), a project of the federal department of education, which rated only 40% of fourth-graders, 33% of eighth-graders and 25% of 12th-graders as "proficient" or "advanced" in math (see the tables and the US equity data *&*).

What is perhaps more disturbing is that the United States spends considerably more per student than the global average and more than developed countries such as Canada, Germany, and Finland that score considerably better. In fact, a 2018 report indicated that "The average US student is almost a year behind the average OECD student in maths education; the average student in Singapore is 3.5 years ahead of her US counterpart" (Rushe, 2018).

And what I find most disturbing is that although the scores of White students are similar to the scores from Finland and would move the United States into a tie for 5th place in science, the scores for Black students are almost 100 points less, similar to students in Cyprus, Moldavia, and Turkey, while those of American Hispanic or Latinx students are slightly higher, roughly similar to students in Iceland and Israel.

Thus, as we know only too well, students in America's public schools who come from groups other than the dominant Caucasian or White population (or smaller Asian population) do not do as well as their dominant culture counterparts. Moreover, even though for most Black students English is the home language, the Hispanic/Latinx students outperform them.

> Do you find these data acceptable?

As Oakes and Rogers (2006) informed us, decades of educational reform have not produced significant changes in these data. We need a different approach—identified here as transformative leadership theory.

Transformative Leadership Theory

As described in the introduction, in 1978, Burns asserted the need for a revolution—a "complete revolution of our entire social system." Transformative leadership has the potential to accomplish such a revolution and now that you have had the opportunity to reflect on its tenets and concepts, hopefully you agree.

Transformative leadership is difficult. Implementing the eight tenets is challenging and sometimes risky. Other concepts, such as developing shared vision, holding high expectations, emphasizing "social justice," or implementing culturally and linguistically responsive leadership, could be added to the eight tenets discussed here. However, if we reflect on and truly understand the tenets that have been identified, we will see that these other ideas are inherent in the tenets already articulated.

For example, shared vision is inherent in the adoption of a mandate for deep and equitable change. Holding high expectations cannot occur unless we consistently reject deficit thinking. And addressing the needs of all students, and creating inclusive and emancipating classrooms, cannot occur unless we attend to culturally and linguistically relevant leadership practices and pedagogies.

Moreover, adopting transformative leadership does not mean a rejection of aspects of other leadership theories and approaches. No transformative leader can act alone, as Angelina's description of her challenges indicated clearly. Hence, aspects of democratic and distributed leadership are clearly needed. Working for the benefit of those who struggle the most or who are marginalized or excluded invokes aspects of critical servant leadership. And of course, the focus on equity and social justice raises concepts from numerous other theories such as social justice leadership, critical race theory, queer theories, and more. It is important to embrace all the strategies and concepts that work for the good of all students.

Integrating the Tenets of Transformative Leadership

In this section, I summarize the eight tenets and their key components, so you have, once again, an overview of transformative leadership theory in one place. Recall that transformation starts with two basic premises or hypotheses that lead to sustainable and permanent change as exemplified by the image of a caterpillar metamorphosizing into a butterfly as in Figure 10.1.

Basic Hypotheses or Premises

1. When students feel marginalized, excluded, worried, and unwelcome, they are unable to concentrate fully on learning. A safe, welcoming, respectful, and engaging learning environment permits students to engage more fully and thus results in higher academic achievement for all students.

Figure 10.1   Metamorphosis.

2. When students are taught about, and prepared for, life in a democracy and for civic participation, then the whole democratic society benefits.

Eight Tenets

These hypotheses are fleshed out in eight tenets that reflect the work of many scholars to explain the basic concepts of transformative leadership.

Tenet One: *The mandate for deep and equitable change (and transformation)*. This requires transformative leaders to know themselves, their school or organizational context, and their communities, to determine where there are inequities and to commit to redressing them. Thus, concepts of vision, context, relationships, and reflection are key.

Tenet Two: *The need to deconstruct knowledge frameworks that perpetuate inequity and injustice and to reconstruct them in equitable ways.* This tenet addresses underlying beliefs and values. It requires courageous dialogue and action that rejects implicit bias, blame, deficit thinking, racism, homophobia, xenophobia, ableism, ageism, and any other "ism" or "obia" that marginalizes or oppresses some groups or individuals.

Tenet Three: *The need to address the inequitable distribution of power.* This tenet recognizes that those who traditionally have held power often continue to exert excessive power and influence and hence that we need to listen to and hear all perspectives and consider each equally. It reminds us to ensure that there are not unintended negative consequences of policies, practices, traditions, and decisions that adversely affect some groups or individuals while they advantage others.

Tenet Four: *An emphasis on both private and public (individual and collective) good* stresses the need to take social and cultural conditions into consideration in the development of policies and implementation of practices that address individual behavior. We must also teach students about, in, and for democratic life.

Tenet Five: *A focus on democracy, emancipation, equity, and justice* requires that equity, inclusion, excellence, and social justice move into the classroom and are considered in the curriculum, the conversations, and pedagogy of the school as well as in institutional conventions and traditions.

Tenet Six: *An emphasis on interconnectedness, interdependence, and global awareness* rejects the common (but false) interpretation of American exceptionalism that asserts everything is the best and biggest in America and thus, that there is little need to understand or be concerned about the rest of the world. It ensures we understand our relationships to, and interdependence with, the rest of the world.

Tenet Seven: *The necessity of balancing critique with promise* reminds us how easy it is to identify challenges and concerns but that we must be committed to addressing them in order to offer hope of a better life lived in mutual benefit of all.

Tenet Eight: *The call to exhibit moral courage* reminds educators of the difficulties and challenges of being a transformative leader. The work is difficult. It calls for fortitude and commitment as there is almost always pushback when one attempts to level the playing field. It requires that we have a strong spiritual sense of our non-negotiables and how we are willing to move forward.

These eight tenets, taken together, provide guidance for truly transforming education in ways that acknowledge a combination of historical forces, present needs, and future hopes.

The Best Hope for an Equitable Future

If you do not take up the challenge of being a transformative leader, who will? We need to be cognizant of the incredible seventh-generation principle of the Great Law of Iroquois Confederacy *&* that dates back over six centuries and is practiced not only by the Iroquois but many Indigenous nations. It acknowledges that because in a single lifetime we have the possibility of knowing seven generations (great-grandparents, grandparents, parents, self and spouse, children, grandchildren, and great-grandchildren), the decisions we make today should result in a sustainable world seven generations into the future.

For Reflection

Think about your ancestors. How difficult was life for your great-grandparents or grandparents? What role did education play? Could more education have improved their lives?

Think about your own family and ask the same questions.

Think about your children. What are they doing now? How well are they doing and what challenges face them? What are your hopes for them?

Think about your grandchildren. What kind of world do you want them to live in? What changes will need to happen? What role could education play?

Can you legitimately say that what you want for your children and grandchildren is what you want for all? This does not imply that you want everyone to attend university or to be a doctor or a teacher, but that you want everyone to be happy, fulfilled, and successful on their terms.

What would need to happen for this to occur?

People often think about the seventh-generation principle as relating to science, ecology, and natural resources, but it applies to every decision, including where to live, what to buy, what to eat, and what policies to enact and support. It should influence all our relationships and decisions, including those we make about education. In fact, tenet six of transformative leadership is directly related to the Native American belief that "we are all related to, and respect, everything in life."

Article 24 of the Great Binding Law of the Iroquois Nations contains the following words:

> The Lords of the Confederacy of the Five Nations shall be men-
> tors of the people for all time. The thickness of their skin shall
> be seven spans—which is to say that they shall be proof against
> anger, offensive actions and criticism. Their hearts shall be full

> of peace and good will and their minds filled with a yearning for the welfare of the people of the Confederacy. With endless patience they shall carry out their duty and their firmness shall be tempered with a tenderness for their people. Neither anger nor fury shall find lodgement in their minds and all their words and actions shall be marked by calm deliberation.
>
> (Constitution of the Iroquois Confederacy, circa 1100)

In the wisdom of these words, you can find courage for moving forward as a mentor and transformative leader. You will need a thick skin. You can act without anger, offensive actions, or criticism. You can be full of *peace* and *good will* and yearn for the *welfare* of all. And you can act with *patience*, *firmness*, *tenderness*, and *calm deliberation*. A Mohawk woman once described to me a beautiful life-size stone sculpture erected in front of a school. It depicted a native woman with seven white doves, depicting seven generations, spiraling around her, the uppermost just leaving her fingertips.

The future is in our hands, but we must work for it. It must also leave our fingertips if others are to benefit. We must join Dr. Angelina M. Walker and other transformative leaders and proclaim with them:

> I will not be silenced into submission. … I will continue to use my leadership and voice to advocate for and ultimately influence educational change.

When we commit ourselves to becoming transformative leaders and work assiduously toward that end, our schools will become safe and caring places in which all students will feel welcome, included, and respected, and able to fully participate in their learning. As this book has argued consistently, the transformation for which we lift our voices is an inclusive, equitable, excellent, and socially just education that embraces and empowers all students to achieve individual greatness to the benefit of civil society as a whole. Let us persist courageously in that task.

Note

1 This does not usually apply to students from East Asian countries such as China and Japan, although South Asian students from India, Bangladesh, and so on, do not generally experience the same successes.

References

Burns, J. M. (1978). *Leadership*. New York: Harper & Row.

Constitution of the Iroquois Confederacy: The Great Binding Law, Gayanashagowa. Circa 1100. accessed June 2019 at https://sourcebooks.fordham.edu/mod/iroquois.asp.

Desilver, D. (2017). U.S. students' academic achievement still lags that of their peers in many other countries, Pew Research Center. accessed April 2019 at https://www.pewresearch.org/fact-tank/2017/02/15/u-s-students-internationally-math-science/.

Oakes, J., & Rogers, J. (2006). *Learning power: Organizing for education and justice*. New York: Teachers College Press.

Rushe, D. (2018). The US spends more on education than other countries. Why is it falling behind? *The Guardian*. accessed April 2019 at https://www.theguardian.com/us-news/2018/sep/07/us-education-spending-finland-south-korea.

Shields, C. M. (2016). *Transformative leadership in education*, 2nd ed., New York: Routledge.

Taylor & Francis Group
an **informa** business

Taylor & Francis eBooks

www.taylorfrancis.com

A single destination for eBooks from Taylor & Francis
with increased functionality and an improved user
experience to meet the needs of our customers.

90,000+ eBooks of award-winning academic content in
Humanities, Social Science, Science, Technology, Engineering,
and Medical written by a global network of editors and authors.

TAYLOR & FRANCIS EBOOKS OFFERS:

A streamlined
experience for
our library
customers

A single point
of discovery
for all of our
eBook content

Improved
search and
discovery of
content at both
book and
chapter level

REQUEST A FREE TRIAL
support@taylorfrancis.com

Manufactured by Amazon.ca
Bolton, ON

25910164R00122